21ST CENTURY CORPORATE CITIZENSHIP

A Practical Guide to Delivering Value to Society and Your Business

Dave Stangis and Katherine Valvoda Smith have undertaken a great service for all of us by laying out the essentials for any company to create both economic and social value simultaneously. How can line management integrate the needs and ideas of all stakeholders into product and service design and implementation? By activating positive disruption and "entrepreneurship inside" our corporations. Nowhere can you find a better roadmap for practical action that provides not only powerful examples and insights but an interactive guide that supports alignment and relevance to achieve the true value of Corporate Citizenship. The authors show that Corporate Citizenship done well enables conventional business success along with increased social and environmental impact. Accordingly, Corporate Citizenship can and should be managed like any other corporate function and doing so successfully can be a vital source of inspiration for all stakeholders. This is a must read for practitioners as well as business leaders.

— *Cheryl Kiser, Executive Director,*
The Lewis Institute & Babson Social Innovation Lab

Now more than ever, business plays a critical role in helping solve some of our world's toughest challenges. Understanding how to create real value that is authentic to the organization's purpose and embedded throughout is critical to enable impact at scale. This book provides fantastic guidance for any business leader looking to make a positive, lasting contribution and transform our world for the better.

— *Trisa Thompson, Chief Responsibility Officer, Dell*

21st Century Corporate Citizenship: A Practical Guide to Delivering Value to Society and Your Business exemplifies the essential truth that aligning the interest of society with a business' bottom line has never been more applicable or beneficial than in the 21st century corporate landscape. This book is a must read for both current professionals seeking to make more of an impact, as well as for students designing their corporate career path.

— *Liz Maw, CEO, NetImpact*

21ST CENTURY CORPORATE CITIZENSHIP

A Practical Guide to Delivering Value to Society and Your Business

BY

DAVE STANGIS

KATHERINE VALVODA SMITH

United Kingdom — North America — Japan
India — Malaysia — China

Emerald Publishing Limited
Howard House, Wagon Lane, Bingley BD16 1WA, UK

First edition 2017

Reprints and permissions service
Contact: permissions@emeraldinsight.com

British Library Cataloguing in Publication Data
A catalogue record for this book is available from the British Library

ISBN: 978-1-78635-610-9

ISOQAR certified
Management System,
awarded to Emerald
for adherence to
Environmental
standard
ISO 14001:2004.

Certificate Number 1985
ISO 14001

INVESTOR IN PEOPLE

CONTENTS

FIGURES, TABLES, SIDEBARS, AND NOTES FROM THE FIELD

FIGURES

TABLES

SIDEBARS

NOTES FROM THE FIELD

We'd like to thank all of the people working in companies who are out in the world doing excellent work every day. We are fortunate that several agreed to share their real-world experiences with us in this book. You can find their stories in the following locations:

FOREWORD

From Denise Morrison
President and Chief Executive Officer
Campbell Soup Company

I am honored to contribute to the foreword of this book with Andy Boynton, Dean of Boston College's Carroll School of Management. *21st Century Corporate Citizenship: A Practical Guide to Delivering Value to Society and Your Business* ties together important principles that have informed and guided my career.

As the CEO of Campbell Soup Company, I work with this book's co-author, Dave Stangis, Campbell's Vice President of Corporate Responsibility and Chief Sustainability Officer, to set our corporate citizenship agenda. I am thrilled Campbell was able to attract Dave, one of the field's most-respected professionals. He is passionately driven to make our company — and the world — better every day.

As a proud alumna of Boston College, I have also followed the admirable progress of the Center for Corporate Citizenship — run by Dave's co-author Katherine Valvoda Smith. My time as a BC undergraduate reinforced the importance of doing right while doing well. Those ambitions and values led me to Campbell, a company that embraces the values of service leadership and promotes them through our Purpose — Real Food that Matters for Life's Moments. Our Real Food philosophy embodies creating real food that is affordable and accessible for consumers, respecting the environment, and innovating to improve the quality of life and well-being of our customers and employees.

Our society stands at the intersection of global consumer demand, technology, environmental sustainability, and human well-being. With markets moving at the speed of ideas, it's difficult to predict where the next disruptive innovation or seismic shift will happen. It is an interesting environment for a nearly 150-year old company with several of the world's most recognized and respected brands. For me, building on the Campbell legacy to develop our 21st century corporate citizenship strategy has reinforced the business and social good that can be realized when we live our Purpose, not only in the short term, but also for generations to come. I believe you can make a profit and make a difference.

This book is important because it offers a step-by-step approach to doing just that — thinking beyond the quarter to nurture the long-term health of the company, its suppliers, and its customers. It helps the corporate citizenship manager consider all the operation's dimensions, methodically assess the operating environment, and develop objectives and a plan to improve both the business and the world.

At Campbell, while our business strategy may shift over time and across markets, our Purpose and commitments to corporate citizenship will continue. We are tremendously proud of our environmental sustainability, public policy, and community achievements, and we know that our leadership differentiates us with many stakeholders.

Will it be difficult? Of course. Will it require time and effort? Of course. But we'll never stop trying to improve. I encourage you, and all readers of this book, to join our efforts, leveraging this invaluable resource. It's the right thing to do for all of us — for our consumers, our companies, our shareholders, and our planet.

From Andy Boynton, PhD
Dean, Carroll School of Management
Boston College

As Dean of the Carroll School of Management, I am pleased to be contributing this foreword alongside one of Boston College's must accomplished alumnae, Denise Morrison. Denise has made important points about the challenges we face and the value of this book in our business context.

21st Century Corporate Citizenship: A Practical Guide to Delivering Value to Society and Your Business is a unique resource for professionals who want to maximize business and social value and who see the opportunity to use the assets of business to solve some of our most pressing environmental, social, and policy problems. Through the work of its Center for Corporate Citizenship, Boston College has been committed for more than 30 years to helping people in companies make more effective social and environmental investments. We've been proud to have Dave as a longstanding member of the Center's Executive Forum and Katherine Valvoda Smith has done an excellent job as its executive director. Their collaboration offers a privileged perspective on the business of corporate citizenship. Dave has worked at the top of his field in three companies and as many industries. Katherine has had the opportunity to observe thousands of individuals across hundreds of companies — and to interact directly with dozens on projects. Between the two of them, they bring almost six decades of insight and experience to this book.

This is an important book for anyone who is just starting out in corporate citizenship and even for more experienced leaders and managers who find they want to or need to refresh their company's corporate citizenship strategy. *21st Century Corporate Citizenship* offers a comprehensive process for how to approach your important work.

Corporate citizenship has evolved quite a bit in the thirty plus years that the center has been in existence. I have seen the profession mature. Even ten years ago, I — and many other management professors — might have considered environmental, social, and policy considerations secondary to business strategy. Today, managing these domains is an essential part of business strategy. Corporate citizenship professionals have tremendously important and challenging work to do. Because the practice is nascent, many companies do not have robust corporate citizenship teams or budgets and corporate citizenship leaders are challenged to both lead these initiatives with little authority and manage processes competently at the same time. This book offers practical insights that help corporate citizenship professionals do just that.

At its heart, corporate citizenship is change management. It is about envisioning a different and better future for business and society. Change management requires the skills of both leaders and managers. Warren Bennis, one of the pioneers of contemporary leadership studies, was fond of saying, "The manager does things right; the leader does the right thing." It's a distinction that should speak volumes to anyone who seeks to both manage and lead in an organization.

Managing and administering are critical tasks: Without them, we wouldn't execute our best ideas and carry out essential functions. Still, Bennis is right. Each of us needs to be a leader, not simply a manager or administrator. We need to not just do things right — which is about execution. We have to also do the right things, which means finding better ways to carry out the missions of our organizations.

As Bennis also said, "The manager administers; the leader innovates." How true. Without leadership, there's no agenda for change and improvement. There's no vision.

In my research, I've developed a list of three things any leader must do to be more than a manager. These reflect my three decades of working with leaders worldwide as a speaker, author, strategy professor, executive trainer, and dean of a management school.

Leaders stake out a clear vision.

It's simply impossible for organizations to do great things if they have no clear expectations of the future. Without a vision, people lurch in different directions. They run in circles. The result is a waste of time, money, and brainpower. Visions focus minds, hearts, and energy.

Leaders get the architecture right.

They design organizations that create the space for talent to soar. At a minimum, leaders remove all of the roadblocks that people must work around to do their jobs. The obstacles could be inadequate information, conflicting goals, mixed signals from the top or confusing reporting relationships.

Leaders call for leadership from every seat.

They make it clear that everyone should step up and find their spots as a leader, regardless of rank, title, or position. This is especially true when it comes to generating ideas.

Because of the magnitude of the challenges and opportunities we face as a society — overpopulation, climate change, inequality, water scarcity — corporate citizenship professionals must be excellent leaders and managers both. This book provides an excellent toolkit to support the important work of our next generation of corporate citizenship leaders — no matter which seats they occupy in their companies.

ACKNOWLEDGMENTS

We would like to thank the many, many people and organizations who contributed to this book. Thanks to Mike Sugarman for suggesting the project and being a great optimist and enthusiast for the field and for the work of the Boston College Center for Corporate Citizenship. To our current bosses (for Katherine, Carroll School of Management Dean Andy Boynton and for Dave, Campbell Soup Company President and CEO Denise Morrison) for their belief in the importance of the project and their support. To our excellent first readers, Steve Quigley, Jessica Shearer, and Kate Rubin, who offered great feedback and ideas. To our Emerald Insights editors, John Stuart and Pete Baker for their patience and advice. To Sara Henry and Liz Rogers for their contributions to the materiality chapter. To all of those who read drafts and offered ideas and insights: Dan Bross, Suzanne Fallender, Rick Pearl, Regina McNally, Marcia Ryan, and James Valvoda. To all of our colleagues who offered "Notes from the Field."

From Dave … to Carolina, Michael, Megan, and Dad for providing the inspiration for, and for instilling, the work ethic and value set to live by. From Katherine … to Ted and Casey Smith for their patience, love, support, and forgiveness for the absent-minded responses to questions, postponed family outings, and evenings at the computer rather than the family table.

To all of our former bosses, who allowed us to disrupt, challenge, persuade, and work above our paygrades (albeit clumsily at times) on the topics and issues outlined in this book. Your faith that we would actually make things a little better than how we found them helped us learn and grow as professionals.

INTRODUCTION

We have always had a strong belief that the science and art of corporate citizenship are fundamental to differentiated business success. This has played out in our personal careers and in the careers and companies we've had the opportunity to influence. As we started to talk about the need for a "how to" book that addresses the fundamentals of corporate citizenship practice, we realized that the two of us had, between us, almost 60 years of experience working in some dimension of corporate citizenship. Though Dave started in environmental health and safety management and Katherine in philanthropy, both of our career paths converged at the intersection of those disciplines and corporate citizenship strategy. As a team, we drafted this book to provide a resource for those in the field — whether you are just starting out, are a more experienced corporate citizenship professional who is rethinking all or part of your corporate citizenship program, or a CEO seeking to get the best out of your corporate citizenship team. We hope you will use this book as a helpful desk resource that can help you think through the solutions that create the most value for your company, your shareowners, and for society.

Dave Stangis is Vice President of Corporate Responsibility and Chief Sustainability Officer for the Campbell Soup Company. Campbell's portfolio of products extends beyond soup to foods such as Pepperidge Farm breads and Goldfish crackers; Arnott's, Kjeldsens, and Royal Dansk biscuits; V8 beverages; Bolthouse Farms super-premium beverages, carrots, and dressings; Garden Fresh Gourmet salsa, hummus, dips and chips; Plum organic baby food; Swanson broths; Prego pasta sauces; and Pace Mexican sauce.

Dave created and now leads Campbell's Corporate Social Responsibility (CSR) and sustainability strategies. As such he oversees the company's execution of CSR and sustainability goals, policies, programs, engagement, and reporting, from responsible sourcing and sustainable agriculture to social impact metrics in the community. Since arriving at Campbell Soup, the company has been named to the Dow Jones Sustainability Indices, the 100 Best Corporate Citizens List, and as one of the World's Most Ethical Companies.

For more than 20 years, Dave has been leveraging corporate responsibility principles to generate business and brand value. Prior to joining Campbell, he created and led the Corporate Responsibility function at Intel. He led a global CSR network organization, a role which gave him insight into corporate citizenship across the world. He's also served on the boards of Net Impact, the Graham Sustainability Institute at the University of Michigan, the University of Detroit College of Business, the United Way of Greater Philadelphia and Southern New Jersey, and Ethical Corporation Magazine. In 2008 and 2013 he was named one of the 100 Most Influential People in Business Ethics by *Ethisphere Magazine*. *Trust Across America* has named him one of the Top 100 Thought Leaders in Trustworthy Business Behavior for four years running.

He earned his MBA from the University of Michigan, his Master of Science in Occupational and Environmental Health from Wayne State University in Detroit, and his undergraduate degree from the University of Detroit.

Katherine Valvoda Smith is Executive Director of the Boston College Center for Corporate Citizenship in the Carroll School of Management. She oversees all the center's activities and strategic ventures, and teaches "Managing Business in Society" in the Carroll School of Management MBA program. The purpose of the center is to help corporate citizenship professionals know more, do more, and achieve more with their corporate citizenship investments by understanding the foundations of how companies create good in the world and add value to their businesses through their environmental, social, and governance (ESG) investments.

The center has conducted research about the practice of corporate citizenship for more than 30 years, developing the deep knowledge and insights that help corporate citizenship professionals manage and improve performance in the ESG dimensions of their companies. The BC Center for Corporate Citizenship supports more than 430 (and growing) members each year; as its executive director, Katherine has had the opportunity to work with dozens of companies and to observe closely the corporate citizenship practices of hundreds of companies and thousands of practitioners.

Before joining the BC Center as Executive Director, Katherine held various academic and administrative positions in higher education and in nonprofit organizations. Throughout her career, Katherine has worked to support several large-scale public-private partnerships and research projects. These include a series of corporate, foundation, and university research partnerships focused on multidisciplinary science initiatives, and on social issues, including education and healthcare. She has also served as an advisor to numerous Fortune 500 companies. She earned her BA from Cleveland State University and her Master's Degree from Rhode Island School of Design.

THE PRACTICAL GUIDE

We spend a lot of time within our own spheres at Campbell and the Center for Corporate Citizenship building models and strategies that deliver results ranging from reputation management to employee and community engagement. We also spend a lot of time providing advice and structured programs to our peers and other companies about how to leverage these disciplines for true business value. We wrote this book to share these perspectives and provide a guide for those who are either just starting out in Corporate Citizenship, CSR, or any effort that touches the environmental, social, or governance (ESG) dimensions of business — or who want to refresh or refine their CSR program.

We want to set a little context upfront about what this book is, and perhaps more importantly, what it's not. First and foremost, this is a book about building a successful business in the 21st century. It's a book about leveraging all the tools, trends, and assets at the disposal of business to drive bottom-line results, value chain resiliency, productivity, innovation, long-term shareowner value, and benefit for the community. We set out to provide a set of practices and checklists that can help you ensure that you are considering ESG impacts and assets to create competitive advantage for your company and a better world for us all. We will use terms like sustainability, corporate responsibility, and social impact to help explain our concepts and translate some of our frameworks, but this is all about creating the most successful business possible in the 21st century competitive landscape.

We initially thought about writing a leadership book, or book on the leadership characteristics needed to run a successful business in the 21st century. But honestly, leadership books are a dime a dozen. Our libraries are full of great leadership books, written by great leaders. They're enjoyable to read and they offer great stories. They offer challenges and improvements to our personal leadership behaviors and help us develop as human beings.

In all of those books, we had not found a simple, and practical "how to" guide for building a comprehensive corporate citizenship strategy anchored in purpose, and leveraging rapidly evolving external environmental dynamics. That's what we set out to do here. You can dive into the examples and resources to any depth you desire. If you work your way through the sections of this book and implement the tools and tactics we offer, you will develop both yourself as an effective advocate for corporate citizenship and your organization's 21st century business strategy will be more resilient, agile, and successful than your competitors.

We wrote this book with several audiences in mind. For the individual corporate citizenship/CSR professional seeking to navigate his or her own meaningful career in the purpose-driven economy; for the CEO who wants to drive real change and agreement among subordinates about the measures of accountability of corporate citizenship; or the board member who wants to know the kind of questions he or she needs to ask to ensure management is paying attention to the right things. All of the profits from the sale of this book will benefit the BC Center for Corporate Citizenship.

THE CORPORATE CITIZENSHIP CHALLENGE

What is corporate citizenship? You may have heard it called a variety of names — CSR, corporate sustainability, corporate responsibility — but all of the terms boil down to the same thing: building a more ethical, resilient, and sustainable way of doing business. In the 1970s and 1980s, Corporate Citizenship, CSR, CR, etc. were a kind of shorthand for talking about corporate philanthropy. As the practice has evolved, so has the purview of the practice. Today when we talk about corporate citizenship, we are talking about how companies exercise their rights, responsibilities, obligations, and privileges in society.

In 1970, Milton Friedman wrote an article in *The New York Times Magazine* titled "The social responsibility of business is to increase its profits." Wildly influential, this article argued that if businesses contributed to charitable causes, they would betray their primary responsibility as businesses: profit-making. Friedman left little room for considering that any ESG expenditures might help a company's profit margins. That was the reigning assumption at the time, but what if Friedman were wrong. What if strategic corporate giving and other ESG activities were not noble wastes of money? What if, instead, they actively created value for the company and society? Since Friedman made his assertions in the 1970s, social scientists have been searching for hard evidence linking ESG performance to financial performance.

They have found a great deal of it; numerous empirical studies have indicated that it does indeed pay to do the right thing:

- An analysis[1] of 30 years of research examining the relationship between corporate social performance (CSP) and financial performance (CFP), looking at 52 studies. It found that the CSP and CFP generally go hand in hand, and this effect holds true across a variety of industry and study contexts. The analysis also suggested that CSP bolsters CFP mainly through improved reputation, rather than through internal benefits such as improved efficiency.

- A 2009 paper[2] analyzed 35 years of research, looking at 214 studies. The analysis concluded that CSP has a positive relationship with CFP — especially if the company can improve its environmental impact and is a transparent and proactive reporter of its ESG performance. In fact, the study notes that companies may under-communicate about their good works and could derive more value from strategic communication.

- An award-winning 2012 paper[3] tracked the market's reaction to an institutional socially responsible investor's engagements with publicly traded target companies. This study looked at 2152 engagements with 613 firms between 1999 and 2009: a very large sample for a study of its kind. The engagements were designed to improve the target company's CSP. Researchers found that when the engagements were successful — resulting in the target company adopting socially responsible ESG practices — the company's share price jumped by an average of 4.4 percent in a year. Unsuccessful engagements had no negative impact on the company's share price. The market rewarded some issues more than others: Successful engagements on issues of corporate governance produced an average one-year abnormal return of 7.1 percent. This figure rose to 10.6 percent for successful climate change engagements.

Although few studies operate on scales as grand as the above three papers, the empirical relationship between corporate ESG and financial performance is consistently documented in current scholarly literature. A 2013 study,[4] for instance, focused primarily on CSR ratings; it aimed to disentangle various measures of environmental performance into a simpler, cleaner metric. Researchers distilled these diverse measures into two principal drivers: the adoption of environmental management practices and reporting, and environmental outcomes (the tangible environmental outputs a company creates). They then investigated the relationship of these to financial performance. They found a significant relationship between environmental processes and financial performance, indicating that firms can create more value by implementing environmental practices and being more transparent. Once again, the data show it pays to be good. Nearly half a century after Friedman's provocative article, the tables have decisively turned. Researchers have, time and time again, demonstrated that socially responsible behavior does not reduce company value.

Today the scope of corporate citizenship touches every aspect of your business. If you don't want to learn something new every day and go home with an ever-expanding to-do list, a career in corporate citizenship may not be for you.

Businesses operating in our global economy have become increasingly responsive to the demands of a range of stakeholders — communities, employees, customers, shareholders, and governments across the world. Many factors have contributed to this trend. The democratization of information and digital and social communication have been major factors. As more people have greater ability to communicate with and about companies across domestic and international borders, there has been a higher expectation placed on companies of transparency and communication with multiple stakeholders. Companies are held to account by greater numbers of stakeholders than ever before and, as a result, they are proactively managing their impacts. As a corporate citizenship manager, it can be tough to make the impact you want. Sometimes your co-workers don't really understand what it is that you do. They may see you as a do-gooder with little business acumen in an increasingly complex corporate world. "Don't you realize we've got financial objectives to meet?" they say. "Why waste time forecasting 10 years ahead when we've got sales targets to meet by the end of quarter?"

There's a seemingly endless amount of red tape and bureaucracy to sort through. Reporting frameworks, Sustainable Development Goals, investment screens, and standards — you could spend all day every day filling out forms if you had a mind to. How on earth do you find the time to *make* the very progress you're reporting on in the first place? What's more, you've no sooner persuaded one area of your company to alter the way they do things than a new executive leader comes in and you're back to square one.

Finally, you may have a CEO asking questions about the annual community golf tournament you've been asked to organize. You find yourself torn between old expectations and driving strategic value. You find yourself wondering how you're ever going to persuade your company's leadership team that there's more to corporate citizenship than philanthropy.

Don't Make This Fundamental Mistake

Sometimes, people working in corporate citizenship think if their initiatives are related to their business strategy, they shouldn't promote the business at all. They can feel confused about the concept of "self-dealing," when a corporate citizenship program is both creating value by improving an aspect of the company, and at the same time doing good in the world. Let's take a look at this assumption for a moment.

First ask yourself if the social or environmental good you achieve with your corporate citizenship investments is less good because your business may benefit also. A number of studies show consumers, employees, and other stakeholders respond much more positively to corporate citizenship initiatives that meet both the strategic needs of the company *and* create good in society.

This means the more logically connected your citizenship investments are to the operating context of your business, the more likely your customers are to accept that your company is committed to doing good. They don't have to work out why you're doing what you do, they just get it and give you credit for being a good corporate citizen.

To make this a bit easier to understand, here's an example of a corporation that's done a great job of connecting their corporate citizenship commitments to their business strategy.

Brown-Forman is a distiller. It's best known for its bourbons, including Jack Daniels and Woodford Reserve. In addition to its whiskey lines it owns Finlandia vodka and also several tequila brands including Herradura and Don Eduardo. For these they need to harvest regular, reliable agave crops. When they moved into this product line they realized they had a problem with managing a consistent supply of agave, which takes a very long time to grow. Rather than thinking about sourcing their agave from independent growers who may or may not have been good stewards of that precious resource — water — in the arid regions of Mexico where they had acquired their tequila brands or moving agriculture elsewhere, they decided to incorporate sustainable agave production into operations. Understanding excellent water management in an arid climate has led to transferrable knowledge that has allowed Brown-Forman to excel at natural resource management and pushed the company to work hard to develop plans to grow their grapes, grains, and agave sustainably. By doing this they've created a more manageable ingredient supply and, because it's grown sustainably, the price and quality remain predictable for them as a business. This move has also enabled them to learn more about water and soil management for all their operations. Given their commitment to sustainable crops it makes sense for some of their most significant citizenship commitments to be related to natural resource conservation. Brown-Forman cites climate change and water scarcity and quality as significant business risks in its annual report and Form 10-K and supports The Nature Conservancy with its corporate giving and employee volunteer programs. These commitments obviously create value for the company and because they do, the company is more likely to invest for longer, which is good for their cause partners. And because Brown-Forman understands the issues related to its business, they're better able to measure the impact of their investments. This mutual reinforcement leads to more value for business and society.

If You're Still Not Convinced About the Benefits of Connecting Corporate Citizenship and Business Strategies, Read This

You know now your corporate citizenship strategy should connect to, and support, the business strategy in your organization — taking into account your company's priorities, growth plan, location, expertise, and community needs. The strategy can be made up of a number of programs and investments across the social, environmental, and governance dimensions of your company's operations.

For the Boston College Center for Corporate Citizenship's *2016 State of Corporate Citizenship* study, we talked to 750 executive respondents. Those who aligned their citizenship programs with their business objectives consistently reported increased success in achieving the outcomes valued by their companies (see Figure 1). Additional independent research also proves alignment and integration help companies achieve success with the following aims:

- Reinforce their brand; deepen customer[5] and employee[6] involvement.

- Address environmental and social issues that have the potential to disrupt their business.[7]

Figure 1: Corporate Citizenship and Business Success

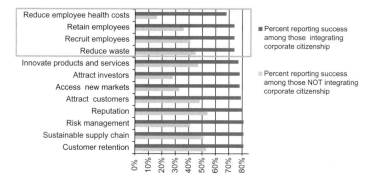

The 2017 BCCCC State of Corporate Citizenship Study Observed That Companies That Do Not Integrate Corporate Citizenship in Their Business Strategy Report Achieving Modest Success in Achieving Business Goals. *Note*: However, companies that **DO** integrate corporate citizenship in business strategy report significantly higher levels of success in achieving the business goals that they set for themselves.

- Assess the impact of their gifts because they understand they are closely related to their business experience.[8]

- Create reputational assets that contribute intangible value to the firm[9] while contributing to the common good.[10]

- Have philanthropic and other citizenship initiatives viewed as more credible as a result of logical connections to the purpose of the company.[11]

In the Boston College Center for Corporate Citizenship's *2017 Community Involvement Survey*, over 90 percent of companies that had connected their corporate citizenship strategy to their business strategy managed to reduce their employee health costs. This was compared with under 30 percent of businesses that had not. And 95 percent of businesses that connect their corporate citizenship strategy to their business strategy have improved their risk management, compared to only 55 percent of those that have not.

Given these results it's not surprising that for the first time in 30 years, executives predicted that the investment in corporate citizenship would increase over the next three years in every dimension queried, including human rights management, philanthropy, recycling, environmental investments, safe products, and employee volunteering.

Why the increased commitment? Because people are increasingly coming to understand corporate citizenship activity contributes to a company's success. So much so that corporations integrating these programs into their business strategy are 2.2 times more likely to gain access to new markets, and 2.3 times more likely to achieve employee retention.[12]

These are incredibly useful facts and figures for you to quote when you're talking to your own executives about your corporate citizenship proposals.

Overcoming Barriers to Strategic Corporate Citizenship

You'd think, given the statistics above, that every company would be implementing citizenship programs that connect to their business strategy. But as you've probably already discovered, there are many reasons why this doesn't happen. Much of this has to do with a lack of understanding about the true benefits that can be gained for both business and society.

Don't get us wrong — there are no "bad" good actions. There are, however, some commonly misguided alternatives to pursuing a strategic approach:

- *Moral appeal*: "corporate citizenship should not be about benefiting the company; it should be about the company doing the right thing." This is a purely charitable motivation, and of course there's nothing wrong with it except that programs created with this aim are at risk of being seen as "extra" because they have no connection to the firm's purpose or strategy.

- *License to operate*: if you're only considering what your community and stakeholders think about you right now, you're defining yourself by where you are today and not where you intend to be in the future.

- *Reputation management*: this confuses social, environmental, and business results with PR. Though there are clearly reputational benefits to good corporate citizenship, focusing purely on reputation leaves on the table other opportunities to create value.

You can see how these rationales don't include any real business reasoning, thereby laying these companies' programs open to executive or customer whims. They focus on the *tension* between business and society, rather than on their *interdependence*. Relying on generic rationales that aren't tied to the specific strategy of the company, they're not sufficient to help identify, prioritize, and address the social issues that matter most.

The more logically connected your corporate citizenship priorities are to your company's strategy, the more authentic and credible your program will be perceived to be by stakeholders of all types — customers, employees, shareholders, and community members — and the more value both your company and society will derive from the investment. Research also shows that when corporate citizenship is aligned with a company's strategy and core capabilities, the company is likely to stick with its investment for much longer and the program will be seen as more credible. This mutually reinforcing loop is a virtuous circle that creates not only a favorable business context, but also the world in which we want to live.

Moving Forward

You know how vital corporate citizenship is to every aspect of the business. Managing the environmental and social impacts of your company and using the assets of business to create value both for the firm and for the world at large is critically important to the future of our environment, society, and economy. It is the way that leading companies are creating competitive advantage today, but some people still just don't get it. It's enough to make an enthusiastic corporate citizenship executive lose confidence.

We believe it shouldn't be this hard. This book is designed to change the conversation for you. You will learn how to do what seems impossible today:

- Persuade everyone from your CEO to your co-workers to line manufacturing staff why corporate citizenship is essential to building competitive differentiation in *all* businesses today.

- Find ways to help executives understand the value of corporate citizenship, so they'll *want* to help drive your corporate citizenship strategy.

- Make changes that stick, instead of reinventing the wheel time and again.

- Prove your worth so you're valued for the benefits you bring to your company.

- Become one of the most influential and respected managers in your business. When you speak, others listen.

Does this sound like a pipe dream? Believe us, it's not. We both have decades of experience in corporate citizenship, and come at it with complementary backgrounds. You'll be getting the benefit of more than 50 years of practical experience implementing programs and driving lasting change in real businesses, as well as industry-leading research. Between us, we've worked with dozens of companies struggling with the same issues you confront and conducted research involving hundreds more. Through this work, we've observed the key factors for delivering value to your company without wasting valuable time and energy.

In corporate citizenship, you're always trying to change things for the better. That's what makes your role so inspiring, but also so challenging. Pretty much all of your arenas involve someone else's job. Want to encourage employees to get involved with your local community? That's HR. Want to reduce the weight of your product packaging to save on transportation pollution? That's product design and distribution. Want to improve the way you report on your activities so your company is considered more transparent and trustworthy by investors? That's finance, communications, and investor relations. You can't do it on your own, so you need to build influence, credibility, and respect at every level throughout the organization. This has never been easy or quick, but you'll find it a lot less onerous with the help of this book.

Integrating your corporate citizenship strategy with the vision and strategy of the company you work in will make your life easier and create the basis for long-term success. We'll show you how to develop credibility so you can enlist people to help implement your program. Soon they'll even be knocking at your door for advice on how to get involved. You'll also raise the bar and achieve a lot more than you'd ever have dreamed of. In time, you'll have turned your company from an "also-ran" to a leader in the marketplace.

It all comes down to one thing: you should not expect your company leaders to invest in corporate citizenship out of the goodness of their hearts. They invest in ideas and strategies because they make business sense. By tapping into that way of thinking, by acknowledging that the way for your work to be valued is for it to add value to the business, you can make all the changes you need without compromising your longer term vision.

There are many books about corporate citizenship, but none like this one. This is a practitioner's handbook, a how-to book, a guide. It's the book that tells you, the corporate citizenship manager and leader, how to navigate your company's waters with a step-by-step map. From creating your corporate citizenship vision and strategy, to working with the different functions of your company, to promoting and reporting on your achievements so you build the authority you need to do it all over again — it's all here. No more worrying about whether you're doing the right thing or focusing on the most important area. This book will help you organize and communicate a clear plan.

So dive in and get started! At the end of each chapter you'll find a handy summary of the main points and a list of questions to answer, to prepare you to move on. The most successful corporate citizenship managers take time to reflect before they move onto the next stage, so we encourage you to answer the questions and challenge yourself to see if you've understood all the issues and that you have a plan for moving forward on each front. It's action, not just thinking, that gets results.

As we noted earlier in the chapter, "corporate citizenship" is called a lot of things; to avoid confusion we're sticking to this one term throughout. Don't worry if your company calls it something different; the semantics aren't as important as what you're trying to achieve. There's a useful glossary of key terms at the back of the book to explain all the confusing terms and acronyms you're bound to come across.

We all know that individuals doing good can make an impact, but with a whole *company*? How much more can you achieve if you harness the power of your entire corporation? The sooner you get started, the more quickly you can make change for the better, make a positive impact in the world, deliver top and bottom-line results for your company, and build your corporate citizenship career at the same time.

You're on an exciting ride — let's get started.

NOTES

1. Orlitzky, Schmidt, and Rynes (2003).

2. Margolis, Elfenbein, and Walsh (2009).

3. Dimson, Karakas, and Li (2012).

4. Delmas, Etzion, and Nairn-Birch (2013).

5. Gardberg and Fombrun (2006).

6. Vitaliano (2010).

7. Simmons and Becker-Olsen (2006).

8. Raffaelli and Glynn (2014).

9. KPMG AG Wirtschaftsprüfungsgesellschaft (2010).

10. Raithel, Wilczynski, Schloderer, and Schwaiger (2010).

11. Thomas, Fraedrich, and Mullen (2011).

12. The Boston College Center for Corporate Citizenship (2014).

SECTION 1

—

LAYING THE FOUNDATION AND CREATING YOUR BASIC TOOLS

1

CONNECTING CORPORATE CITIZENSHIP TO BUSINESS PURPOSE

What's the purpose of the company you work for? Stop and think about that for a moment. Why was it originally created, even if that was many years ago? This can be an interesting question to ask, and a difficult one to answer. There's a very good reason to make the effort. In the process of exploring these issues, you'll learn how to design a corporate citizenship strategy and program that is relevant, comprehensive and — most importantly — that works. This in turn will enable you to become more knowledgeable and successfully influential within your company.

All successful businesses were created originally to fill a market need or solve a societal problem. This is the core of the purpose. The purpose of your company could have been to make life more convenient, to provide something essential, or even to create an exciting experience. Depending on how long your corporation has been around it may still be providing that same solution; alternatively, the company may now be selling products and services that address problems that did not exist at your founding with solutions that were unimaginable. At its core, a successful company delivers something to the world that only it can provide in its distinctive way. It's a special point of differentiation from its competitors. Purpose is the reason your company exists. It is related to vision and precedes strategy. When you have your company's core purpose clear, it should guide your corporate citizenship.

Let's look at some sample company websites to better understand the concept of purpose (Table 1).

Table 1: Company Business Purpose

This is the Company's Purpose	This is How They Realize Their Purpose
"3M is a global innovation company that never stops inventing."	"Over the years, our innovations have improved daily life for hundreds of millions of people all over the world. We have made driving at night easier, made buildings safer, and made consumer electronics lighter, less energy-intensive and less harmful to the environment. We even helped put a man on the moon."
"Campbell Soup Company's purpose: Real Food That Matters For Life's Moments."	"For generations, people have trusted Campbell to provide authentic, flavorful and readily available foods and beverages that connect them to each other, to warm memories, and to what's important today."
"McDonald's reaches customers with enjoyable meal experiences wherever they are."	"McDonald's is innovating new tastes and choices, while staying true to customer favorites. Modern service. Personal engagement. Great-tasting burgers and fries. Building on our commitments to our people, our communities, and our world."

The purposes of the example companies have changed relatively little over time. It's the *way* they realize their purposes that's evolved, as their operating contexts have changed over the years.

It's not always easy to uncover this core purpose, but if you can get it right you'll have a solid foundation that provides the justification and boundaries for your business strategy and corporate citizenship program. What's more, unlocking a company's core purpose can unleash many new ideas, helping you to think more imaginatively and broadly about how corporate citizenship can contribute to your company's purpose and unique ideal. Your company's purpose is here to stay, representing the value it provides to your customers year after year. It's not a program or a campaign, it's for life.

Think about Ford Motor Co., for example: the business was originally created to provide affordable transport for everyday people, and it still does that today. Ford changed its business model to adapt, like all companies do. It went from mass-producing a single model in a single color, to customizing individual models and features and vehicle types (sedans, coupes, trucks, hybrids). In today's sharing economy some consumers either can't afford or aren't interested in owning a car, but they still want to be able to use one from time to time. So Ford has developed partnerships with technology companies, and now leases vehicles to ride-sharing systems as well as selling them to individual owners. The company is still true to its original purpose of giving people an affordable way to travel from place to place, just not in exactly the same way it used to.

We mentioned McDonald's in our examples above. Their original purpose was to serve fast, family-friendly meals on the go, to the increasingly mobile society of mid-century America. When McDonald's was founded people ate out less, mainly at lunch and dinner; McDonald's therefore came up with the solution of burgers and fries. They've interpreted that purpose across both decades and geographic regions. As work hours became longer and more women worked outside the home there was higher demand for meals on the go at different times of day, so McDonald's developed a popular breakfast menu and expanded its service hours. In the United States, the breakfast menu is so popular that McDonald's now serves breakfast all day. McDonald's expects to have more than 450 restaurants in India by 2020,[1] and none of them serve beef. You can see how they've interpreted their purpose through a changing context and applied their core competencies (replicable inventory and fast, easy preparation) to new contexts; if they had thought about their company purpose as "getting customers fast bur-gers," they wouldn't have had the flexibility to apply these skills to changing times and environments.

After all, in the 1950s and 1960s "fast, affordable, family-friendly meals on the go" were defined very differently to how they are today. In those days delivering hot, tasty, and consistent burgers and fries from clean stores, being supportive of the community with gifts in kind, and supporting the local little leagues, was sufficient to fulfill their purpose. But as consumer expectations changed over time and geography, and as their business grew, McDonald's had to maintain their core competencies in menu planning, purchasing, and training, and add new ones in nutrition, wellness, and environmentally friendly packaging. Now they have wellness initiatives for families to understand better the nutritional profiles of their menu items, and offer training and development to employees (Warren Buffett has called the company a gateway to future employment). Their commitments have changed as their context has changed, but their purpose has not.

WHAT THIS HAS TO DO WITH YOU

Why is your company's core purpose of any concern to you? You want to set up environmental programs, develop an employee volunteerism strategy, and help your organization use its assets to do more good in the world.

It's important because if your strategy, programs, goals, and metrics aren't tied to your company's purpose and strategy, you lose the opportunity to reinforce the purpose and support the strategy. How can you expect to get resources and enlistment to execute if you're not advancing your company's purpose and strategy?

If you bumped into your CEO or another senior executive in the hallway, could you explain what your business is trying to achieve right now, with what resources, and who's involved? Could you name the stakeholders who have a say in all this (the people affected by the strategy, such as employees, customers, suppliers, and investors)? Would you be able to identify your corporation's key customers, what investors think about the company, and how easy (or otherwise) it would be to engage employees to act on your corporate citizenship vision?

If you couldn't do this, you're not alone. Most people in your company wouldn't be able to, even if they were at a very senior level. In fact, after you've worked through this chapter, you'll be more knowledgeable about your own firm than most anyone else in it. How's that for a great start?

BUSINESS PURPOSE, VISION, AND STRATEGY

By the way, if you're wondering what is the difference between a company's purpose, vision, and strategy; it's this: purpose is the motivation for all it does; vision is a vivid, easily communicated image for how the world will be different if it's successful in achieving its objectives; and strategy is the plan of action for how it will compete in the market to achieve this vision. Purpose is the reason you're undertaking your strategy, and usually doesn't change. Strategy changes as customers, consumers, and markets evolve. Later on we'll look at strategy in more detail; for now, just know that it springs from your corporate purpose.

HOW DOES YOUR CORPORATE CITIZENSHIP PROGRAM SUPPORT YOUR COMPANY'S PURPOSE AND STRATEGY?

Your company has a core purpose, and so does your corporate citizenship program. Can you describe what it is? How would your company's customers describe it? What would your employees say about it? How about your suppliers, investors, and other stakeholders?

You can sit in your office and ruminate on this, or you can tap into the wisdom of co-workers — just interview them. Ask what success would look like for them. Their words are important here, as they will likely use different terminology than you. A fellow employee they might say, "I love coming to work because what this company's doing is making a real impact." An investor on Wall Street would never say, "Well, it's great they have a robust volunteer program." They may, however, note your company has a low staff turnover and does a great job of managing its people. Can your program contribute to that strength? Data tell us there is a strong positive correlation of volunteerism and employee engagement with low turnover, so you probably do contribute to the Wall Street investor's assessments of the quality of management and stability of the company.[2]

To inspire people you need to paint a vivid picture of your corporate citizenship strategy, and how you intend to fulfill and measure it. At this stage, you're simply collecting information; imagine you have a pile of "corporate purpose" on your desk, and a stack of "what I'm going to do about it." You also have a collection of words and images to describe your purpose to the people that matter.

You should be able to describe success from your perspective, but much more importantly be able to describe it also from the CEO's perspective, from the board of directors' perspective, from the CFO's perspective, and from the chief HR person's perspective, etc. Getting these people on board with your program and how it advances corporate purpose and strategy is what will make your corporate citizenship program stick and be sustainable in the long term.

WHAT MAKES YOUR COMPANY UNIQUE?

Remember when we talked about what makes your company different and special at the beginning of this chapter? You may have wondered what this means for the corporation you work for.

Notes from the Field

. . . .

Purpose as True North

Shannon Schuyler is Principal, Chief Purpose Officer and Corporate Responsibility Leader at PwC and President of PwC Charitable Foundation

Corporate citizenship — both as a guiding principle and as a structured program that companies employ continues, as it must, to evolve. At our firm, like many, we began with philanthropy then developed a formal Corporate Responsibility (CR) program and more recently focused on shared value.

To keep up with the unprecedented pace of change and stay socially and business-relevant, companies must identify ways to leverage their core strengths and capabilities to deliver impact at the intersection of business and society. The most highly effective corporate citizenship integrates the firm's purpose, values, business operations, and CR activities to drive positive change and deliver scalable impact. Ultimately, the scale of a solution is what matters most. Not how much or how many, but how broadly and deeply.

As a global financial services firm with teams of experts working on the development and deployment of fin tech solutions, including block chain (digital or cryptocurrency), we recognized a unique role for PwC in addressing a serious global problem: the lack of speed, low transparency, fraud, and waste associated with disaster relief efforts. The disaster

---

recovery market is a vital resource for people all over the world: there are more than 140 million victims of natural disasters every year (http:// reliefweb.int/report/world/annual-disaster-statistical-review-2014-numbers-and-trends) and while there is always a strong outpouring of financial support to help those affected, roughly six to up to 20 percent of all money allocated for disaster relief is lost to inefficiency and corruption (PwC "Cryptocurrency disaster relief consortium" — Development Launch Plans — Power Point presentation/May 2016; and "Fact Sheet" provided to Megan Discullio by Paul Dunay in May 2016).

The proprietary block chain and smart contracts technology we were developing for our clients (a decentralized ledger that enables anyone in the network to view any and all transactions from the transfer of funds to the transport of supplies) could also revolutionize the way that humanitarian assistance is managed during natural disasters. We created our Cryptocurrency and Disaster Recovery & Relief Solution (CDRC) as a pilot effort to test our unique prototype, refine the solution, and harness an emerging technology to solve a critical social issue. Our CDRC service is a more effective way to ensure that donated funds get to the right places and are used for the right purposes — enhancing transparency and trust. The effort reflects our purpose, which is to solve important problems and build trust in society, engages our people in meaningful work that can have visible and broad impact for multiple stakeholders, and demonstrates the capacity of business innovation to drive systemic change.

Thus applying PWC's distinctive strengths and expertise to meet a global need and build resilience in society delivers economic, social, and environmental impact and shifts our perspective from "doing good works" to working for the greater good.

There are thousands of service companies, hundreds of food companies, and dozens of automotive companies and airlines, but it's what they each do differently from the others that gives them their competitive advantage — their differentiation. Are products offered faster? Are they more innovative? Do they offer unique or more features? Are they less expensive than competitors? It's not just *what* they provide ... it's *how*!

What makes your product or service special? If you're a retailer, you may describe your stores as the most welcoming place in the world to shop for high-end goods. Your shoes may be the ultimate in low-priced but high-fashion items — or you may employ a buy-a-pair/give-a-pair strategy. To determine what makes you unique sounds simple but it can be really hard to answer; even large leadership teams sometimes have a difficult time answering this question.

HOW DO YOU DIFFERENTIATE YOUR CORPORATE CITIZENSHIP PROGRAM?

Maybe you have the best R&D people in the world, or possibly your ability to deliver a particular experience is second to none. These are your firm's core competencies — the things you do exceptionally well as a business and which differentiate you from your competitors. Your purpose and your competencies come together to make up your value proposition. And just like with your purpose, you now need to be able to describe your complete value proposition so that anyone in the company would say, "Oh yes, that sounds just like [your company name]." They get it. They understand what you deliver and what you do in a more unique and compelling way than anyone else.

Just like defining your business purpose, it's difficult to do this on your own. You need to talk to people in your organization to understand how they see things. You'll get different opinions from different people, and your job is to pull them together and identify common themes. This is an iterative process; don't expect to get it exactly right the first time.

Using this process, you'll get a better understanding of how your corporate citizenship program should be implemented so that everybody understands it belongs to your company, and no-one else can do it quite like you! We'll look at some specific company examples of this in Chapter 4 when we discuss strategy.

MAPPING YOUR BUSINESS PROCESS FLOW

Now that you understand your purpose and core competencies, we're going to get more granular. This is the time to map your company process flow, so you can see the areas you want to touch or leave alone with your corporate citizenship work. In order to define the building blocks, tactics, risks, opportunities, and link to strategy, you need to think about the flow of your business. This involves understanding the material flow, the intellectual flow, and the value chain from beginning to end. You also need to consider the human capital flows. Who sets your company strategy? Who develops new product? Who delivers or manufactures what you are selling?

What do we mean by flow? Take food and beverage companies, for example. They grow (or purchase from growers) products which are harvested, distributed, and processed in order to make the food they sell. A food company also has an R&D department to create new recipes, which links to the production process. Their sales team sells the products in their portfolio to retailers, supported by the marketing and branding functions. At the end of the chain, consumers load the foods into their shopping carts as they cruise the supermarket aisles. In addition to all this, there are other functions within the business that touch each part of this process: human resources, finance, procurement, legal, and so on.

Perhaps you're a service provider, maybe a large consulting firm or a government agency. You still have a supply chain and need to distribute something; it could be intellectual property or consulting services. Just like the food manufacturer, you're delivering a product or service and have many processes which allow this to happen.

A useful trick for creating a map of your business flow is to look at it from the viewpoint of one of your stakeholders. How would your customers describe it? How would an investor describe it? Or how would another employee see it?

From a corporate citizenship perspective, every element in this flow will illuminate opportunities and challenges. These line and support functions could have human rights implications, environmental impacts, activism issues, or energy and water requirements. When you look at the business flow, you'll find the levers you can pull to create or enhance your citizenship program. There may be too many to include in the first pass, although by mapping it out you're uncovering the risks as well as the opportunities for your work (Figure 2).

CREATE YOUR MAP

Now that you've talked to key people and better understand the business flow, you need to pull all these pieces together in a way that makes sense to you. Use whatever format works best; it could be a tree with branches, or a simple flow chart. Try not to get bogged down in the structure and format. Mapping out your business flow can get really complicated, and you're unlikely to capture every last detail. Just make a start.

By creating this map, you'll learn a lot about the business, possibly more than you think you need to know. This will prepare you to be vastly more informed and valuable as you progress through the company.

We're going to cover the main functions of your business in more detail in later chapters. For now, just think of your map as an outline of the arenas of operation that you should consider in your planning.

Figure 2: Business Process Flow, Campbell Soup Company

AGRICULTURE
• Building strong relationships with local and regional farmers
• Conducting research and engaging farmers to help conserve and protect water resources, reduce energy use and greenhouse gases, and enhance soil quality, leading to higher-quality ingredients and products

SUPPLIERS
• Standards and expectations set for supplier performance
• Supplier scorecards and assessments
• Purchasing high-quality ingredients produced by local farmers and key suppliers
• Supplier engagement in sustainable agriculture and packaging initiatives

MANUFACTURING
• Leading systems and technology for ensuring quality and safety of ingredients and products
• Global objectives set and investments made in energy and water conservation, alternative energy, and waste management and recycling

DISTRIBUTION
• Logistics optimization to improve environmental impact and distribution of finished products to retail customers
• Innovation from packaging to shipping to reduce transportation costs
• SmartWay℠ certification of our shipper fleet

CUSTOMERS
• Support of and partnership with customers on CSR and sustainability initiatives and priorities
• Sharing of best practices and strategies from suppliers through customers
• Participation in the Sustainability Consortium

CONSUMERS
• Sector-leading consumer insights and recognized leadership in consumer affairs
• Advancing nutrition and wellness across the portfolio
• Balancing demand for quality, affordability, and convenience with sustainable packaging

COMMUNITIES
• Strong relationships with our hometown communities and their residents
• Engaged employee volunteers linked with strategic social impact programs, informed by community needs and designed to make meaningful and measurable impacts

YOUR COMPETITION

You've thought about your company's purpose, vision, strategy, process flow, core competencies, employees, and customers. Before you move forward, you need to look at your competition again from the corporate citizenship perspective.

You may think of competitors as businesses competing in the same product or service sector as your own, but there are many different ways to compete. It's especially important to define your competition according to the key risks and opportunities in your business. For instance, there may be risks and opportunities in your supply chain which you've positioned yourself to deal with differently than your competitors. Or you might have some unique competitive advantage or disadvantage in distribution, sales, or communications.

Let's consider it from the perspective of a food company. They may want to help their consumers understand nutrition and personal health via an app that will lead to more informed food choices. They would then be competing with fitness apps in the technology sphere, not just other food companies.

From a business perspective alone, never mind corporate citizenship, you could be competing with almost anyone. If your company wants to recruit the best and brightest employees, you can help the HR department become better at recruiting by creating an engaging, inspiring workplace. When you know who you compete with — and in what arenas — you've begun to build a framework to differentiate your corporation from the competition.

From a corporate citizenship perspective, you could have a competitor that is outside of your sector because they're competing with you on the ethical nature of their supply chain. It's also important to consider your competition from the standpoint of reputation. If you were to walk around your local community and ask people who your competitors were, they might say the local hospital, university, or nonprofit, because they're viewing you all as members of a single community rather than as members of disparate industries. If you are asking financial analysts about your competitive set, they will likely be assessing you against companies in the same industry, offering the same (or similar) services. If you are asking your HR leaders, they will be looking at companies across industries (and very likely geographies) to attract the best talent possible to your company. Understanding who your various stakeholders view as competitors is an important undertaking.

The world of competition is starting to look very different now, isn't it?

If you've worked through this chapter and are able to answer the questions below, congratulations. You're well on your way to mapping the foundations that will support a comprehensive, 21st century corporate citizenship strategy.

WHAT WE'VE COVERED

- Company purpose, and why it's important
- Why your corporate citizenship program needs to connect with that purpose
- The difference between business purpose and strategy
- How to create your own corporate citizenship purpose
- Your business process flow: what it is and why it's important
- How to work out who you're competing with

10 QUESTIONS TO ANSWER BEFORE YOU MOVE ON

1. What is the core purpose of your business? Do you know how your customers, and society in general, would describe it?

2. Can you describe what long-term success looks like for your business? Is this view consistent across your organization?

3. Does your vision of success paint a picture, describe a feeling, and evoke value for your employees, customers, and other stakeholders?

4. Have you mapped out your business process flow?

5. Do you understand the risks and opportunities within the flow?

6. Have you identified elements of your current or planned corporate citizenship program that can help mitigate risks or achieve opportunities?

7. What are your company's core competencies (what it does better than any other company on the planet)?

8. Can you identify elements of your corporate citizenship program that do not connect to your purpose and/or core competencies? How might you rethink allocating the resources that these efforts consume?

9. Do you know who your competition is within both industry and reputation contexts?

10. Do you know how you compare to each competitor in each context?

NOTES

1. http://www.thehindu.com/business/mcdonalds-india-to-double-out-lets-by-2020/article7648207.ece

2. The Boston College Center for Corporate Citizenship (2015).

2

CREATING ADVANTAGE IN YOUR MARKETPLACE

Now that we've looked at business purpose, let's turn to the marketplace. Corporate citizenship is very much about building relationships, and there are many interested parties who would love to influence what you're doing. This can be difficult to manage, but at the same time can be of enormous help when you're developing your strategy. The more effectively you engage with these stakeholders, the more leverage you will have with them as you implement your corporate citizenship strategy.

This chapter is about how to determine which key audiences in your marketplace to engage, and how to turn them into allies and resources as you implement your corporate citizenship strategy. We'll look at customers, activists, employees, and investors, as these are groups you'll need to understand and engage with if you want to be an influential player in the corporate citizenship space. Employees are a particularly important stakeholder group. We'll talk more specifically about them in Chapter 3.

CREATING ADVANTAGE WITH YOUR PRODUCTS AND SERVICES

Who do you "speak to" out there in your marketplace?

One of the first groups you probably thought of is customers, but let's define what we mean by customer. When we mention famous brands such as Intel, Nike, and Coca-Cola, you probably think of them as being "business to consumer" companies, but virtually all companies apart from retailers (whether online or not) sell to other companies, and not direct to consumers. For products like Coca-Cola, that means supplying distributors and grocery retailers, not the general public directly. For the purpose of this chapter we're defining customers as the *first purchaser* in the value chain. Companies clearly market to their end consumer, but understanding the needs and interests of your first primary customer is critical to creating value with your strategy.

Your initial step is to identify your customers, and then to prioritize them. Not all customers are created equally; some have more value to you than others. If you're in the consumer products sector in the United States, for example, one of your largest customers is likely Walmart or Amazon. You might also have strategic partners, or customers you're trying to grow from small to large. Consider your key customers or customer segments and create a prioritized list. You could base this on size or influence, although you might also consider factors such as geographic areas where your business wants to expand, customers who are growing the fastest, or even customers who best align with your strategic focus. Your sales and marketing department should be able to help you with this.

HOW CUSTOMERS RELATE TO WHAT YOU PRODUCE OR PROVIDE

The products and services you sell have an impact on society far wider than their actual usage. This ranges from the actual impact (the environmental, human, or societal impacts of what your company produces) and the perceived or realized impact (views held by your customers and consumers).

If you're a manufacturer, this impact is tangible, and you can see it playing out every day all across the world. Sugar taxes imposed on soft drinks in various countries, and the debate about whether advanced pharmaceutical drugs should be made available in undeveloped countries, are just two examples of how products are not just products in customers' eyes — they're bundles of ethical and cost issues. This presents both challenges and opportunities for you. Re-thinking how you source and deliver products can lead to a host of different ways to approach things. Consider the simple yet transformational reduction in laundry detergent package volume and weight that developed from the decision to create a more concentrated product in order to ship less water, at lower volume/weight and therefore lower carbon intensity and transportation costs. This is a great example of an improvement, driven by the efforts of big box retailers to reduce shipping cost, maximize shelf space, and manage natural resources, which has brought both increased profit and environmental benefits.

For decades, the performance regulations companies had to deal with in the corporate citizenship space were all "you shall not" — you shall not emit so many pounds of this, you shall not dispose of so many tons of that.

As time went by, companies grew accustomed to working with these guidelines, and in fact many businesses began to move faster than regulatory frameworks to improve environmental performance. In recent years, the worlds of regulation and voluntary standards have moved toward a disclosure mindset — in other words, to be competitive, businesses are expected to provide customers — and sometimes the general public — with information so that they can make their own purchase or "enforcement" decisions.

Dealing with disclosure regulations versus performance regulations may sound less daunting. As a corporate citizenship manager, the focus on disclosure rather than performance can make it more challenging to drive action within your company than if the performance improvement was compulsory. People feel more compelled to act when you say, "We need to change how we do this because there's a law against it," than they do when you say, "We need to change how we do this because we're required to disclose how we approach a certain issue." This is certainly the case with relatively new disclosure requirements such as climate change risk disclosure in the 10K (the U.S. listed companies' regulatory filings), conflict minerals, or slavery and human trafficking (for any business that operates in California). Expect to see many more types of "disclosure" regulation in the future as customers and the general public demand and grow accustomed to ever increasing product transparency. So, this is where much of the work you do to build excellent internal relationships comes into play.

You may wonder about products where there is an ethical or sustainability component, such as those labeled eco-certified, fair-trade, organic, and locally sourced. While the number of products and services for which customers are willing to pay a sustainability or ethical sourcing premium remains limited, that number is growing as consumers look for a different kind of marketing promise. Companies and consumers alike want to buy from companies they believe represent their personal values, even if they're not always willing to invest more for the privilege. So the overall messages you send about actions you take on corporate citizenship issues do impact your company reputation (which has a financial value) and sales.

Notes from the Field

. . . .

Leveraging Your Company's Core Competencies in Corporate Citizenship Strategy

Christopher T. Lloyd is Executive Director, Public Policy Development & Corporate Responsibility at Verizon

At Verizon, we know that consumers and global activists are prepared to use the power of the Internet and social media to hold companies accountable for delivering community value. The genesis can be found in the 2008 global economic crisis that demonstrated unilateral business models that extract resources from communities, and only deliver value to business owners and shareholders, are not sustainable. It was during this crisis of confidence that consumers and stakeholders signaled to banks, extractive firms and manufacturers, among others, that businesses need to provide value to the community in exchange for a continued license to operate.

Expectations for shared value creation have led Verizon to think about solving the daunting challenges facing the world in ways that generate significant business and social value. Last fall the United Nations published a list of the 17 most pressing global priorities in the form of the Sustainable Development Goals (SDGs). Each SDG describes a social challenge that represents a market opportunity. Entrepreneurs are building lucrative and sustainable businesses by addressing these challenges, and instinctively using technology as the core to problem solving. We have overlaid our corporate citizenship strategies on the SDGs as a way to strengthen understanding and impact.

The Internet of Things (IoT) — that is, ubiquitous connectivity, the cloud and big data analytics — can be strategically applied to solve problems. By connecting almost anything to the Internet processes can become smarter, greener, and more efficient, thereby scaling solutions and delivering societal impact and value.

At the core of this type of entrepreneurial innovation are entities such as Hahn Family Wines that has partnered with Verizon on a project to increase agricultural yield in drought-stricken California. The winery is using an IoT solution to optimize grape harvests. Management receives data regarding soil and air conditions from wireless sensors in the ground and data analytics convert the data into actionable information to help determine when to irrigate, helping to reduce water use and operating costs.

By looking at social challenges as market opportunities and applying technology to transform data into information, Verizon is helping Hahn Family Wines and other tech-savvy entrepreneurs gain new information about solving social problems and are creating sustainable business models that generate value for society and for business.

BUILDING A SELF-ASSESSMENT STRATEGY

Disclosure-based regulation has forced many businesses to look into their supply chains to build self-assessment strategies. In fact, a whole new consultancy profession has emerged to help corporations manage this (maybe it's even a potential career opportunity for you). Disclosure-based regulation drives a different set of behaviors than performance-based regulation; so this is an emerging area you need to learn about and understand.

There are disclosure guidelines and standards set up for most sectors to manage performance tolerances. For example, you have probably heard of ISO9000, which was the original quality management system. There is also SA8000 for responsible workplaces and social standards, ISO14000 for environmental management systems, ISO26000 which sets a framework for corporate citizenship and social responsibility, and the Global Reporting Initiative (GRI). These are all resources to help manage and monitor work and to define the standard of practice or production. These exist for corporate citizenship and we will discuss them in greater depth in Chapter 9.

WHAT DOESN'T KILL YOU MAKES YOU STRONGER: WORKING WITH CHALLENGING STAKEHOLDERS

So who are your stakeholders? They're groups such as suppliers, customers, and employees. You can also add external groups such as competitors, members of the communities where you operate, values-based investors, issues advocates, regulators, activist groups, and policy-makers.

Most large companies attract a wide range of advocates, activists, and values-based investors (more about the investors later). There's a widely used acronym that covers most of their areas of interest: ESG. Historically, the first impulse of business people, at least in the United States, has been to dismiss stakeholders with ESG concerns as anti-business, anti-market, anti-progress socialists who don't understand the power and importance of market forces. This response represents a lost opportunity, because if you dismiss the chance to hear from your nonfinancial stakeholders, you can't learn from them. In today's world of citizen journalism and social media, thinking of those who call for accountability from institutions as fringe is no longer practical. These stakeholder groups can gain traction and support quickly.

Ask yourself, what issues are most important to each of these stakeholders? You probably have a sense about the most pressing issues in your marketplace already. However, different stakeholders will have different priorities. Many are single-issue focused — organizations we would normally think of as activists, or advocates for a cause. They wake up in the morning and it's deforestation; they go to bed at night and the issue is still deforestation. Every time you talk with them, it's always about deforestation. So while you're trying to manage multiple issues from a corporate citizenship perspective, they're trying to get you to focus on *their* one thing. They may have had a relationship with your business based on that single topic for many years, and while they may sometimes be challenging to work with, they can also be the most helpful in identifying how their issue will impact your business long term.

Somebody — in other words, you — has to step into the role of Issues Manager. This means monitoring emerging ESG trends and taking the initiative to seek out the single-issue activists that most people would rather not engage with. It can be intimidating to talk with groups whose primary role may be to criticize what you do as a business, but if you go out and meet these people and really try to understand what makes them unhappy, you'll often find places of common ground. It's far, far better to have a relationship with an activist organization that's willing to speak to you privately than for them to launch a public campaign against you. Not only that, you'll have the advantage of tapping into their own intelligence, which will help you see around those corners we mentioned earlier.

Remember, if you want to be a leader in corporate citizenship you don't just need to manage this process, you need to *leverage* it so you're the best in your sector — even the world. You need to create a competitive advantage out of the thing that looks like trouble to other companies. You may be the one person in your organization who really understands the activists' agendas, so the information you're gathering is extremely valuable both to you, in corporate citizenship, and your business. Engaging these groups can also enhance the work your company or industry association is doing to establish norms and standards of practice to address complex social and environmental issues such as sustainable consumption and climate change.

How so? Part of your job is to identify issues and spot the things you're not dealing with today, but will likely need to manage in the future. Most ESG issues have a fairly predictable trajectory; they're quiet to begin with (which is when we tend to ignore them), they ramp up over time and get attention, especially on social media. It should be obvious that the early part of the curve is the best time to engage and start to leverage the relationship; by the time the issue has escalated, reaching a tipping point while making national news, it's too late. You'll just look defensive.

If you're a huge corporation, you and your CEO need a credible, well-oiled reputation with global governments around the world. You certainly don't want him or her asking you why activists are protesting outside your shareholder meetings, about a topic that wasn't even on your radar. There's not a company in the world with a famous brand name that is not engaged in emerging ESG issues right now. They do it either because they're forced to do it, because they want to do it, or because it gives them a competitive advantage. The choice of *how* you engage is yours.

An example of this is how the U.S. food sector is engaged in the controversial subject of GMOs, or Genetically Modified Organisms. This topic has been simmering in the United States for decades but recently reached a boiling point, with broad debates across the industry, on social media, in State laws and ballot proposition and eventually resulting in Federal legislation signed by the President in July 2016. Campbell's Purpose informed the company's response to this set of issues. Since its founding, the company had been committed to providing wholesome food to families. The evolution of agricultural technology has introduced, along the way, issues that could not have been anticipated by the company's founders. In each case, however, the founding purpose informed the company's response. Campbell executives had been monitoring the topic for a few years and were the first major food company to call for national, mandatory labeling of GMOs on packaging — a move which was disruptive within the food sector.

Leading the market to a new way of doing things is not often easy. Another example of this is from the automotive industry, parts of which have been racing to produce hybrid or electric vehicles to increase their competitive advantage. Toyota's launch of the Prius would not have predicted the success Toyota has experienced with the model over the last 20 years. In 1997, Toyota released the Prius in Japan and then released it worldwide in 2000. The Prius Prime responds to the advances in battery technology and allows for a plug-in.

Initial testing in the United States, in 1999, before release to the general public nearly derailed the Prius before its debut. The few drivers involved in the testing were less than impressed. When the car was first released in the United States, performance was lacking; the Prius took 13 seconds to go from 0 to 60 mph and the transition from electric to gas power was not smooth. Subpar acceleration combined with an untested market for the Prius, almost halted plans to sell the car outside of Japan.

Toyota in the United States had to do some hard negotiations with Toyota Japan to get the price down to one that the soft U.S. market would accept. Toyota had to modify the vehicle's design to meet expectations of more discerning buyers in the United States, like more horsepower, better interior finishes, etc. Environmentally conscious buyers and a handful of vocal celebrities like Ed Begley promoting the idea of alternative fuel vehicles prevailed and the Prius caught on. Toyota had to respond to the market after testing, but it also had to lead the market to hybrids. Today, Toyota cars account for more than 70 percent of all hybrid cars in the United States,[1] which is the second largest hybrid market in the world after Japan. Tesla's entry into this market and its partnership with Solar City promises further disruption for the industry.

Notes from the Field

. . . .

The Role of Companies in Public Policy Debate

Dan Bross, Senior Director of Corporate Citizenship and Executive Director of the Microsoft Technology and Human Rights Center (Retired) Microsoft

Corporations have a responsibility to their shareholders, communities, and employees to participate in the public policy process to enhance business and shareholder value.

The question is not — "should corporations participate in the public policy process" but rather — "how do corporations participate in the public policy process."

Corporate participation in the public policy process is an important means of enhancing the business and social value that companies deliver and is fundamental to free and democratic societies. Microsoft participates in the public policy process in countries in which we have operations around the world. That participation is focused on public policy issues that are core to our business and important to our stakeholders. We believe our engagement serves our business interests and also creates stronger, more informed public policies.

Our engagement in the public policy process is grounded in and guided by our unwavering commitment to strong corporate governance.

Louis Brandeis is famously quoted as saying, "sunlight is the best of disinfectants, lamplight the most efficient policeman." At Microsoft, we believe strongly that a corporation's public policy advocacy should be fully transparent. Our engagement is outlined in our annual global Public Policy Agenda that is available on our corporate website. The priorities identified on that Public Policy Agenda are based on our assessment of current and emerging national and local laws and regulations.

Five fundamental principles inform our policies and operational practices:

1. Transparency in Public Policy Advocacy.

2. Compliance, Accountability, and Transparency in Political Spending.

3. Empowering and Support Employees.

4. Oversight and Transparency of Trade Association Contributions.

5. Responsibility in Governance and Reporting.

In the United States, we work to advance our policy agenda by: (1) supporting a government affairs programs designed to educate and influence elected officials on key issues directly related to our business; (2) supporting candidates both directly from corporate funds (where allowed by law) and from funds contributed by employees to the Microsoft Political Action Committee (MSPAC); and (3) membership in industry and business trade associations and coalitions.

The Regulatory and Public Policy Committee of the Microsoft Board of Directors is responsible for overseeing the company's public policy work and receives regular updates and briefings on Microsoft's public policy engagement.

I started my career in the political and activist arena — working for equity in access to healthcare for those suffering from HIV/AIDS. In my time in those roles and at Microsoft, I've seen some of the most important issues of our society addressed effectively by companies: education, marriage equality, immigration, and human rights to name just a few. The companies involved actually became leaders in the movement to address these issues. Corporations are, ultimately, communities of people working together towards shared objectives. Both individual citizenship and corporate citizenship are required to solve the biggest problems of our time.

IF YOU CAN'T DIFFERENTIATE, COLLABORATE

Sometimes it does not make sense to forge ahead alone to lead the pack due to lack of resources, expertise, or executive buy-in. Other times you may have missed the leadership position on a particular issue that will continue to be material to your business operations. In those cases, it is often better to collaborate with others in your industry to address the issue either through tactics including voluntary standards, codes of conduct, supplier training, and others. This is sometimes referred to as pre-competitive "collabotition" or the practice of collaboration with competitors to achieve mutually held and undifferentiating objectives. Industry organizations like the Electronic Industry Citizenship Coalition (EICC), the Forestry Stewardship Group (FSG), and many others exist to help companies work through issues material to the whole industry efficiently.

MANAGING THE PROCESS

So how do you stay on top of all this? As a corporate citizenship professional, you'll spend a significant amount of your time dealing with activists and advocates, so the sooner you come to terms with this and find ways to use it to your advantage, the better. To get started, create a list of your main stakeholders, identify their potential issues relative to your company, then create a list of priority issues. You could organize it by topic, functions in your business, or regulatory changes happening around the world that could potentially have a negative impact on your business. Are there developments in Asia, for instance, that could be an early warning of what could happen in your country, or vice versa? In Europe GMOs were required to be labeled long before the United States, so this is an example of a change in one geographical area that diffuses to another market. Large companies operate globally and what happens in the EU is likely a precursor to what happens elsewhere. For example, starting in

2017,[2] EU Directive 2014/95 affects any company or organization (undertaking) operating in an EU member state with the following attributes:

- More than 500 employees;

- Are "public-interest" organizations, which are defined to include EU exchange-listed companies as well as some unlisted companies, such as credit institutions, insurance undertakings, and other businesses selected by Member States (based on size, number of employees, and/or activities);

- A balance sheet total of at least EUR$20 million (approximately USD$25 million) or a net turnover of at least EUR$40 million (approximately USD$50 million).

This directive requires that all member states establish guidelines for disclosures on sustainability social and environmental factors, with a view to identifying sustainability risks and increasing investor and consumer trust. in order to take account of the multidimensional nature of CSR and the diversity of the CSR policies implemented by businesses matched by a sufficient level of comparability to meet the needs of investors and other stakeholders as well as the need to provide consumers with easy access to information on the impact of businesses on society. This push toward transparency will certainly have an effect on the disclosure practices of companies all over the world.

Another example is animal welfare. Treating animals in a humane way is one aspect of this, yet the topic also feeds into product labeling and other areas such as cage-free chicken or crate-free pork. Already, companies are shifting their positions on subject such as antibiotic-free meat, or even plant-based proteins taking the place of animal proteins. Some of these issues may not have yet reached the burning issue stage, yet they need to remain on your radar. When do you expect these issues to become business-relevant, and how could they impact your business and customers? We'll look at the process for tracking stakeholders and issues in Chapters 3 and 4.

You also need to recognize how difficult it would be for your company to change operations or processes in order to leverage these developments. This means building an internal communications system that enables you to share issues with decision-makers in your organization so they too can start considering alternatives ahead of a crisis. It could be via a newsletter that goes out once a week or month, talking about the hot ESG issues you're watching on the heat map, analyzing other companies around the world currently experiencing challenges in this area, and explaining how your business is — or might be — prepared to ward off such trouble. This will help you communicate the right information to the right people, including your government affairs team, those who decide where to locate manufacturing facilities, the purchasing department, and other relevant players.

By setting up a regular communications channel you're not only building collaborative relationships with those who could otherwise mobilize against the company; by doing so you are elevating your potential influence as the person who's helping the corporation be proactive and stay competitive. You represent a tremendous information asset, and will be a go-to colleague when peers confront continually emerging controversial issues.

CREATING ADVANTAGE BY WORKING WITH VALUES-SCREENED INVESTORS

Investors in your business come in many shapes and sizes — institutional, private, socially responsible, values-based, and ethical. It's the larger institutional investors with a socially responsible ethos we'll focus on here. As a group they file hundreds of shareowner resolutions each year related to ESG topics. These resolutions demand better disclosure of corporate activities that run the gamut ranging from political contributions, environmental or supply chain activities, remuneration, or governance structures and practices just to name a few topics. Investors may ask whether there's sufficient gender or racial diversity on your corporation's board, or how easy you make it for shareowners to access board meetings. In recent years these proposals have been gaining a lot of traction, as well as higher vote tallies.

Just as with issues-based activists, so it is with values-based investors. If you're not paying attention to them, you'll not be managing a relationship, and you will potentially be responding to a resolution.

With this in mind, almost every large company has adopted a strategy to engage with large values-screened investors and analysts on a periodic basis. Intel was one of the first companies to do this formally back in 1998, which resulted in it earning recognition and credibility with social investors. As a result, by 2003 Intel stock had become the largest holding in socially responsible mutual funds in the world.[3] Why did Intel go to all this trouble? Because these values-based investors see a high level of ESG performance as indicative of a company's long-term success; engaging with them meant Intel could build a win-win relationship. Values-based investors can often serve like your external partners from a corporate citizenship perspective. They care not only about the financial success of your business, but also about the long-term ESG assets of your company. Corporate citizenship leaders and managers can work proactively with their investor relations teams to identify and develop strategies for addressing "hot" issues.

So how can *you* replicate Intel's success? Set up a scheduled meeting, just like we talked about with the activists, but this time between yourselves and the investor groups that are focused on environmental or social governance. Your aim is to educate them about what you're doing and listen to their concerns. Intel found this process created significant trust, and also generated a wealth of information and market intelligence which helped inform their future strategy.

There are many ways to stay linked to this group of values-based investors beyond having face-to-face meetings. You can monitor shareowner resolutions online, and find out the resolutions other companies in your sector have already been faced with. Resources include U.S. SIF (the Social Investment Forum), ICCR (the Interfaith Center for Corporate Responsibility), and PRI (the Principles for Responsible Investment). These are just a few of the groups that monitor and track long-term issues that values-based investors are thinking about. For instance, as we're writing this book, the CEO of Blackrock (one of the largest institutional money managers in the world) has just sent a note to hundreds of CEOs asking them to place more focus on ESG topics. It's an area where changes are happening on a daily basis.

PULLING IT ALL TOGETHER

If you're like many corporate citizenship professionals, you might underestimate the level of work involved in creating advantage in your marketplace. You have to meet with key customers, activists, and investors, research what they're doing, map out what's going on in their world, and inventory and compare your initiatives and goals against these issues. Once you've done that you need to share your findings internally in a way that your company's decision-makers can understand which will also cause support for your company and corporate citizenship program. It's not complex, but it is important.

With your B2B customers, the conversation will revolve around seeking to understand what they're doing from a corporate citizenship perspective, and how you as a key supplier can help deliver that for them. In the same way that you're being strategic about your own program, you're also being clever as you find out the relevant information, then communicate it so it can be used by the right people at the right time within your organization, as opportunities arise. For example, if you're an insurance provider with skills and knowledge in workplace wellness, you might help your corporate clients create their own health and wellness programs. If you're a food manufacturer, you could work with your customer to develop sustainable packaging so they achieve their own sustainability targets more easily.

With activists related to your sector, you want to demonstrate that you are willing to engage with them to seek a win-win scenario. With values-based investors, meetings will demonstrate to them how seriously you take their concerns and long-term viability of your business.

All these actions are like currency with your customers, activists, and investors. They add value for them, and strengthen your relationships with them. This doesn't happen by accident. You need to make these strategies and tactics part of your action plan.

WHAT WE'VE COVERED

- Looking outward to your marketplace; key groups to consider are:

  - Customers;

  - Activists and advocate groups relevant to your industry;

  - Values-based investor groups.

- Knowing who your most important customers are is the first step toward building good relationships with them.

- When you are a supplier to your customers you can help them with their sustainability goals.

- Attentive engagement with hard and soft regulatory bodies can create advantage for your business.

- It's important to work with issue-based groups in a proactive way, so you prevent problems and possibly even develop a competitive advantage from the relationships.

- Creating a heat map of issues that could affect your corporation is a great way to keep track of status and current priority/importance.

- Working with, rather than against, values-based investors means your company benefits long term.

10 QUESTIONS TO ANSWER BEFORE YOU MOVE ON

1. Have you identified your key customers either by importance of relationship, importance to your business, or influence over your success?

2. Have you identified other key stakeholders? Have you identified and do you understand their key issues?

3. Do you know who is responsible for monitoring, communicating, and managing emerging issues within your company? If it is you, do you have a process for doing so? If it is a colleague, do you have a regular update process in place?

4. Has your business sought out activists that either have a negative opinion of you, or want you to change some aspect of what you do?

5. If you are a publicly traded company, do you understand who your shareowners are and how values-based investors factor into your holdings?

6. Have you started to monitor shareowner resolutions of ESG issues that could affect your business? How are you using this information to your advantage?

7. Do you understand the impact of disclosure-based regulations or transparency in general on your business?

8. What are your customers' key corporate citizenship strategies? What are you doing to help advance them?

9. How are you working with your own suppliers in order to advance your own corporate citizenship agenda?

10. What are you asking your suppliers to do or not do, in order to advance your customers' corporate citizenship strategies?

NOTES

1. U.S. HEV sales by model (1999–2013).

2. http://eur-lex.europa.eu/legal-content/EN/TXT/?uri=CELEX% 3A32014L0095

3. Research Magazine (2003), Intel Corporation (2004).

3

OF THE PEOPLE, FOR THE PEOPLE, BY THE PEOPLE

You likely understand by now that your best results will come from working with and through the people in your organization. Your success is also dependent on engaging with professionals outside of your company, such as investors, customers, suppliers, communities of operation, and the representatives of natural eco-systems. All of these people — both inside and outside of your company — are your stakeholders, which we will define as any group or ecosystem that can impact or be impacted by your business.

Your stakeholders are the primary audience for what you do, so understanding them is critical. If you don't know who you have an effect on, and who might impact you, it's difficult to have a clear picture of your business strategy or value chain. Take a minute to list your stakeholders.

STAKEHOLDERS ARE THE REASON CORPORATE CITIZENSHIP PROGRAMS CAN'T BE A ONE-SIZE-FITS-ALL

Stakeholders exist in a hierarchy. One of the most well-established sustainability frameworks recognized represents this hierarchy, for example, we must have a healthy environment to have a healthy society; we must have a healthy society to have a healthy economy.[1] Think of your stakeholders as an anchor point, the context for your corporate citizenship program. Everything starts with them — and your stakeholders are not only individuals, they include the environment and its ecosystem services on which we depend to live, multiple sectors of our society, and of course, customers, employees, and the myriad others upon whom we depend to maintain a successful business.

Building on the example provided in Chapter 1, McDonalds' business purpose has always been to provide tasty, affordable meals and experiences to families on the go (remember, business purpose doesn't change). But as they've expanded geographically, and because they've always considered their customer experience in broader terms rather than just through the lens of their burgers and fries, they've always been able to apply this purpose across the world in ways that are appropriate for that local market. In India, for instance, they don't serve beef because of religious observances, but they're still basing their business on their core competencies: limited menus that are quickly prepared and offered to their customers fresh.

Part of the secret of their success is that they've adjusted their strategy to accommodate their customers' expectations, not only across geographic boundaries but also over time. Back in the 1970s, consumer desires were for lots of food for their dollar, whereas now they are for healthier choices.

So how did this actually come about? The interesting thing is that at the beginning of the public health discussion around obesity in the United States of America, it was mainly the media that was leading the discussion, rather than consumers. McDonalds at the time was purchasing more apples and lettuce than any other restaurant chain in the country,[2] but even so their reputation as a place where consumers could choose a healthy meal was being damaged. So they adjusted their corporate citizenship program to meet those consumer expectations, and became a leader in this area. This also led to them rethinking their supply chain. Not only were they now purchasing larger quantities of fruit and vegetables, they also proactively reduced their packaging (remember Styrofoam clamshell boxes?), because they determined that they could lead consumers to discard less into landfills and reduce litter.

This is a great example of how a corporate citizenship strategy has been changed to suit the needs of its customers depending on where and when they live. McDonalds made these strategic changes because it has never taken a "one-size-fits-all" approach to its stakeholders; on the contrary, it has an effective corporate citizenship team monitoring their stakeholder landscape long term, identifying what their customers want from them often before they're fully aware of it themselves.

HOW YOUR AUDIENCES AND STAKEHOLDER GROUPS AFFECT YOUR BUSINESS VALUE CREATION

Each group your corporate citizenship program comes into contact with has an effect on the plans you create, how you implement them, and the kind of value you generate for your business as a result. Table 2 shows the main stakeholder groups and illustrates how each one can affect the success of your strategies.

EMPLOYEES

Employees are critically important stakeholders for all companies. After all, companies are abstract entities that are comprised of multiple covenants and contracts. One of the primary contracts is the exchange of labor for currency. The relationships of employees to the company and the power balances can shift over time and circumstance, but the relationship must always be

Table 2: Stakeholder Salience Analysis

(a) List Potential Stakeholders	From the Perspective of the Stakeholder				From the Perspective of the Company				
	(b) Legitimate Claim on the Company (0–7)	(c) Company Influence on the Stakeholder (0–7)	(d) Urgency (0–7)	(e) Sum of b + c + d	(f) Legitimate Interest in the Stakeholder (0–7)	(g) Stakeholder Influence on the Company (0–7)	(h) Urgency (0–7)	(i) Average of f + g + h	(j) Sum of (e + i) Divided by 2 = Salience Score
2. Ingredient growers	3	7	5	5	7	7	2	5.3	5.15
4. Employees	5	7	7	6.3	7	6	5	6	6.15
5. Environment	5	3	6	4.7	5	5	5	5	4.85
6. Customers	7	7	2	5.3	7	7	3	5.6	3.5
7. Community Garden Association	2	1	7	3.3	1	3	0	1.3	1.5

Table 2: (*Continued*)

(a) List Potential Stakeholders	From the Perspective of the Stakeholder				From the Perspective of the Company				
	(b) Legitimate Claim on the Company (0–7)	(c) Company Influence on the Stakeholder (0–7)	(d) Urgency (0–7)	(e) Sum of b + c + d	(f) Legitimate Interest in the Stakeholder (0–7)	(g) Stakeholder Influence on the Company (0–7)	(h) Urgency (0–7)	(i) Average of f + g + h	(j) Sum of (e + i) Divided by 2 = *Salience Score*

managed. For example, think about a high-tech company's stakeholder relationships. Recruiting highly trained people and keeping them engaged would be one of their most important outcomes for creating business value. To do this they might give their employees more flexibility, better work—life balance, benefits, or increase their diversity and inclusion efforts; but they could also provide the opportunity to take part in corporate philanthropy and volunteering projects.

Through these activities, not only will employees gain new skills and broaden their perspectives, they'll also feel more motivated and loyal to the company. What's more, if the corporate citizenship program is well integrated with efforts by HR or and the Organizational Development function, they'll be able to develop their leadership and other professional skills. As a result, the employees who take part in the corporate volunteer program will be more engaged, productive, and less likely to look for jobs elsewhere, and the company will benefit from increased levels of teamwork. This will both save on recruiting costs and improve productivity.

Conversely, an industry with large numbers of lower wage workers (and high staff turnover) may get fewer benefits from volunteer programs that require a lot of time away from work. For a business like this, a more effective activity could be to organize a single "all hands" day of service that raises awareness of the company's commitment to its customers. Alternatively, a gift-matching program could increase staff engagement and loyalty, and might be a better choice.

Ages and Stages

Employees at different ages and stages of their careers often want very different options from their employer. This necessitates creating multiple ways to participate in your corporate citizenship program; a one-size-fits-all approach does not work typically.

There has been a lot written about the expectations of "Millennials," sometimes referred to as "Generation Y" and "Generation Z" (those employed beginning around the year 2000): many companies assume these groups are more socially conscious than others, although research at the Boston College Center for Corporate Citizenship around employee participation in company corporate citizenship programs does not bear this out. What we do see is that networking opportunities, especially when they involve high-level executives, are the most significant motivator for them to participate in corporate citizenship programs. This makes sense when you consider younger professionals are just beginning to develop their networks. Also, given they're more likely to have more time than money at this stage, it's obvious why they prefer to volunteer rather than to give money to causes. Professional development and learning new skills while rubbing shoulders with company leaders is a great fit for early stage career professionals.

Mid-stage employees, on the other hand, although also very motivated by recognition and networking opportunities, are more likely to be time-constrained. This "sandwich" generation is squeezed on the one side by parenting and on the other by responsibility for aging parents. They're likely to be attracted by corporate citizenship activities that include their families.

Finally, later career workers are often eager to demonstrate their experience and establish a legacy. The opportunity to be a mentor and recognized for their achievements can be very important to them. They want to leave their company and their world in better shape than they found it, and to be recognized for their leadership, as one of the people who made this happen.

Notes from the Field

· ·

Going Glocal: The Value of Local Perspectives in Global Corporate Citizenship

Tom Tropp is Corporate Vice President, Ethics and Sustainability for Arthur J. Gallagher & Co.

Arthur J. Gallagher & Co. plans, designs, and administers a full array of customized, cost-effective property/casualty insurance and risk management programs globally. Our company operates in 32 countries with over 23,000 employees; half of whom are in the United States with the rest across the globe. We are reminded regularly that the core values we celebrate in the United States overlap with the core values each of the other cultures of our corporate family. During my last trip to New Zealand, I was reminded of the broad impact of our corporate citizenship as an expression of those values.

New Zealand is one of the most beautiful and inspiring places on earth. There are strong movements in progress to honor the rich heritage of the land and of the people and our "Kiwi" employees have taken prominent places in those efforts.

On the North Island there is an ancient seabird sanctuary that had become inhospitable to birds. Invasive nonnative plants and rodents had reduced nesting and endangered bird populations. To restore the habitat, continuous maintenance of nesting areas is required. This is no small project. Our employees have taken on this project and work regularly to clear invasive plants, clean out nesting boxes, and erect "signal gates" that indicate nesting birds. It is a difficult work performed on the side of a mountain at steep angles; and our people love it.

So what was the impact of this project in a remote area of a country on the other side of the globe from our headquarters? Our communication folks published the story so that employees around the world might get a glimpse of the project. The idea was simply to share the message that working for the environment is a value that we embrace. But the ripple effect went far beyond what we anticipated.

The story generated more interest than expected. I think there were a few reasons for this. Our team in New Zealand are new additions, joining us as a result of a recent merger. Many of our other employees had little knowledge of that country, and this was a chance to get to know the lovely home of new colleagues. Because we showed strong support from our corporate office, our colleagues in New Zealand saw that we value them and that they are part of a global family.

I believe that most significant result of this project was that it showed that a value that seemed unique to one country is, in fact, appreciated and duplicated by colleagues in other parts of the world. While laws vary among the 32 countries in which we operate, our values extend across those borders. When we demonstrate a commitment to human rights, to the environment, to serving the poor, to any cause, we affirm that it is our people who make the difference. No matter where we live, we share common values and when we expand the shared values of the firm beyond the balance sheet, we give our employees another reason to appreciate and stay loyal to our company.

CONSUMERS

In the same way your corporate citizenship program is not a one size fits all for your employees, neither is it for consumers. Research shows consumers will often claim that they make purchase decisions based on the environmental and social attributes of products. However, this is far more likely to be the case for indulgence purchases than for staples. When buyer behavior is observed (rather than attitudes) the research shows time and again that most consumers continue to make choices based on price, quality, and convenience, and on whether the item was good for their families or saved money.[3]

Consumer research shows that brands and companies with the strongest consumer affinity are those with a clear purpose and compelling social value. Moreover, consumers are likely to shift purchase decisions away from companies that they feel have done something wrong (polluted, treated employees unfairly). Consumers may not pay more for green or conflict-free products, but they'll demonstrate their loyalty when they believe the values of the company align with their own. Understanding where your consumers stand and how your product is perceived is vital. This is a difficult balancing act for companies. Your corporate citizenship program can help demonstrate your company's commitment to important issues and stakeholders.

You may have heard the terms "cause branding" and "cause marketing," so it's worth making the distinction clear. Cause branding is a company's commitment to promoting awareness about a cause by using their brand assets, as Pampers did when they advised parents on the front of their diapers to put their babies to sleep on their backs rather than their stomachs, which helps prevent Sudden Infant Death Syndrome. Cause marketing is when a company creates an ethical call to action, as Pampers also did when they donated a vaccine for every pack of diapers sold.

INVESTORS

The more sustainably a company is run, the better its long-term prospects. It's able to attract and retain employees more efficiently, has superior enterprise risk management, and is less vulnerable to a consumer or media backlash. This results in a lower volatility for the investor and potentially better long-term returns.

However, only a small number of investment analysts and firms measure how a company is performing regarding sustainability, supply chain management, disclosure, or governance (although there is a much larger group of analysts who see the corporate citizenship profile of companies as a proxy for good management). Most institutional investors examine ESG data only in binary terms, considering whether the company engages in responsible environmental or social practices in a "yes or no" kind of way. They may ask whether there's a CSR report, whether the company has measurable dimensions for its corporate citizenship activities, what board representation (diversity, in all senses) looks like, and whether they have a sustainability committee. As corporate citizenship practices mature it is inevitable investors will start to compare one company against another in a more analytical, detailed, and deliberate manner.

A recent notable instance of this came when Larry Fink, CEO of investment company BlackRock, wrote in February of 2016 to the CEOs of BlackRock's portfolio companies to assert the need for better long-term thinking among corporate executives.[4] As the CEO of one of the largest asset management companies in the world, Fink's letter earned wide media attention. Among the topics he covered in the letter,

> ... *Generating sustainable returns over time requires a sharper focus not only on governance, but also on environmental and social factors facing companies today. These issues offer both risks and opportunities, but for too long, companies have not considered them core to their business – even when the world's political leaders are increasingly focused on them, as demonstrated by the Paris Climate Accord. Over the long-term, environmental, social and governance (ESG) issues – ranging from climate change to diversity to board effectiveness – have real and quantifiable financial impacts ...*

SUPPLIERS

The more sustainable your company's suppliers are, the more value they provide to you as a customer, and the more this improves your ability to forecast as well as your business resilience. A good example is an agricultural producer who works hard to sustainably manage water reclamation and soil management. By increasing resilience in the agriculture system they're able to sell their ingredients at more stable prices, which in turn helps their customers forecast their purchases more reliably. They've created a win-win situation.

If your company has a strong corporate citizenship program you'll also likely offer your codes of conduct to your suppliers, so they can be trained on corporate citizenship practices as well. We'll go into procurement in more detail in the next chapter, but for now it's worth understanding how important it is for your suppliers to be given the opportunity to improve their own performance along similar dimensions. Your suppliers should be fully informed of and on board with the commitments that your company has made to issues like sustainable sourcing, safety, and human rights. Part of your citizenship program may be getting suppliers support and training to meet your corporate citizenship commitments. We've seen from some of the human rights and safety problems in recent history such as the Rana Plaza factory collapse of 2013 that even companies very peripherally connected to the apparel manufacturing facility experienced fallout from their real or even only perceived affiliations. Managing your corporate citizenship through the value chain is critically important.

GOVERNMENT

The government exerts significant control and influence on corporate practices and processes. If your company does not engage in solid environmental and community programs, or adhere to voluntary standards, it's more likely to become subject to regulations in the future. This is especially true if you're developing products that require a large amount of natural resources, or are potentially harmful. This is not limited to companies who manufacture products that could be seen as damaging in their own right; take the low-cost fashion supply industry described above, for example. It produces a fairly innocuous product, clothing, but there are multiple opportunities for labor abuse which could attract unwelcome government attention if proactive corporate citizenship strategies aren't applied.

Corporations that take action ahead of regulation are less likely to experience government or legal interference later on; this in turn increases their revenue potential and decreases the risk of rising costs that are outside their control.

ENVIRONMENT

Sometimes we forget that although ecosystems can't speak to us directly, NGOs can give them a voice. We need a sustainable and healthy ecosystem in order to support a healthy society, and we need a healthy society to support a healthy economy. Imagine three concentric circles, with the outermost ring being the natural environment, the middle ring being the social environment, and the inner ring the economic environment. We need the outer two in order to create the third as is illustrated in Figure 3 in this book.

So you can see from this chart how your corporate citizenship program must be informed by, and have a benefit for, each of your stakeholder groups. It begins and ends with them, creating a virtuous circle of value along the way. Take a moment to think about your own company's stakeholders and how your program would relate.

Figure 3: Spheres of Sustainability

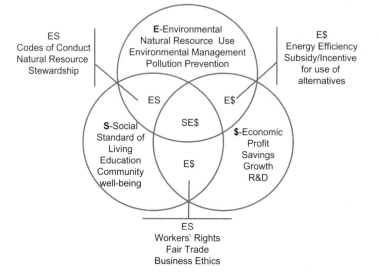

(a) **Spheres of sustainability and their interconnections**. The areas of intersection represent varying degrees of sustainability and the indicators of sustainability for each domain area. The greater the area of overlap, the stronger and more resilient the domain of sustainability. Ideally, all three domains overlap to ensure complete sustainability as in panel (b).

Spheres of sustainability

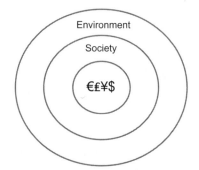

(b) **The interdependent relationship of our environmental, social, and economic ecosystems**. We must have a healthy environment to have a healthy society. We must have a healthy society to have a healthy economy. A healthy environment is the foundation of all prosperity and social wellbeing. *Source*: (a) EPA Sustainability Concepts in Decision-Making: Tools and Approaches for the US Environmental Protection Agency 2012.

HOW YOUR CORPORATE CITIZENSHIP PROGRAM CAN AFFECT YOUR STAKEHOLDERS

Companies often overlook that they have capabilities that are distinctive to them, through which they can positively impact a social or environmental problem in ways no other company can.

One example is The Disney Channel. Disney has an enormous media footprint, especially with kids and families. So they've started working with evidence-based messaging targeted at those same kids, for causes like reducing bullying or improving body image and confidence for young girls. This has included developing storylines in their network TV programs about how it's ok to be an individual (so the top line message isn't necessarily about bullying, it's a subtler message about respecting differences). These themes run through all of their "tween" programming. They are embedded in storylines, and encourage children to celebrate their individual strengths and to stand up for what they think is right. The message is clear: the brave and heroic thing to do is to be kind and accept each other's individuality.

In this way the Disney Channel's corporate citizenship program is having a positive effect on children and on society as a whole — not only in their environmental commitments and philanthropy and employee programs, but also through their programming. And the benefit for Disney is enhanced brand value, as parents and children respect it all the more for these positive messages.

Always look for opportunities not only to receive good from your stakeholders, but to do good for them as well. There are many ways to implement projects that may not bring short-term benefit, but provide natural opportunities for you to do good in the course of your "regularly scheduled programming" as Disney has demonstrated. In the long run, they'll add to your company's reputation and relationship with your customers and other interested stakeholders.

STAKEHOLDERS BEFORE ISSUES

When determining which issues to focus on, it might seem like corporate citizenship professionals should start with the hot topics — the ones with the biggest media buzz. This can work well, but only if your company actually has a set of stakeholders who are affected by these issues, or who can work with you to positively impact outcomes. Your focus must be congruent with stakeholder interests.

What could go wrong if you were to focus on issues not aligned with stakeholder interests? You might find yourself being influenced by issues getting the most public attention right now, but which are not necessarily the ones most meaningful for your stakeholders or business strategy. You could run the risk of investing in programs that aren't positively impacting the people you're most concerned about, or the contexts you're most trying to influence.

Remember when we talked about embedding corporate citizenship strategy within your corporate strategy in Chapter 1? Your stakeholders are a key part of your strategy — they're what brings it to life.

All stakeholders are not created equal, in that some groups have a greater ability to influence (or be influenced by) your actions and program. Stakeholders may rise or fall in importance over time. Prioritizing stakeholders and issues is a continuous process. Relationships and issues shift over time, and a group that was not as influential or whose issues were not as urgent yesterday may change position (seemingly overnight if you're not monitoring all the time). You should establish a discipline of review to assess:

- *Influence*: How capable is this stakeholder of affecting your program?

- *Urgency*: What is the degree to which stakeholder claims call for immediate attention?

- *Legitimacy*: How great is your impact on that group
  or resources that they need? How valid are their arguments and
  demands?

Twenty plus years ago, Ronald Mitchell and his colleagues developed a managerial approach to stakeholders. A lot has changed in
20 years and we've adapted this model to reflect the process by
which we think stakeholders should be prioritized today. Those
stakeholders that have a legitimate claim on your business — those
who are impacted most by your operation and or on whom you
depend to make your business successful — should get priority
attention. Those who have influence are prioritized as a group to
watch and stay in touch with. This group is tricky to manage as
they possess some power that may allow them to affect your operating environment. Those who have urgent issues — which may or
may not relate to your business but whom you could help would be
prioritized next. Think here about communities affected by natural
disasters. Any community affected by natural disasters will have
urgent needs. If the community affected is not among your arenas
of operation or markets, you might limit your level of support
because that particular event is urgent, but does not legitimately
connect to your business. Those who possess more than one of the
attributes described above should get higher levels of attention
depending on the combination of attributes (Figure 4).

There are so many issues in the world today and so many stakeholders who are advocating for worthy causes, that you need a way
to prioritize which you can target for attention. In our experience
the most efficient way to prioritize issues is to think first about the
stakeholders. Issues belong to stakeholders and if the stakeholder is
important to you, it is likely that their issues will be, too.

Take a minute to prioritize your stakeholders. Here are some examples of how stakeholders might be prioritized based on their attributes.

Legitimacy, Urgency, Influence = 7 (if you are a consumer brand,
consumers with concerns about ingredients who have the attention

Figure 4: Stakeholder Prioritization

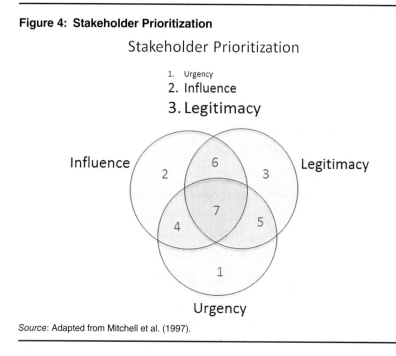

Stakeholder Prioritization

1. Urgency
2. Influence
3. Legitimacy

Source: Adapted from Mitchell et al. (1997).

of media or another significant communications platform like social media might fall here).

Legitimacy, Influence = 6 (executives with specific priorities, standards organizations, or codes of conduct organizations might be prioritized at this level).

Legitimacy, Urgency = 5 (if you are a consumer brand, consumers with concerns about ingredients or supply chain issues, but with no access to key players in the industry or media might fall here).

Influence, Urgency = 4 (well-organized NGOs with specific campaigns that have low connection to your business might be prioritized at this level).

Legitimacy = 3 (suppliers who contribute to the creation of your product or service would have a minimum ranking at this level — it can rise at any time with the addition of another attribute, but it will not fall).

Influence = 2 (general interest media might fall here, as might executive colleagues).

Urgency = 1 (smaller or unrelated advocacy groups that have significant issue concerns unrelated to your business would fall here).

Sometimes it is difficult to disentangle these attributes to figure out which stakeholders should be prioritized for attention. Here is one methodology that you can use to track and prioritize stakeholders. To assess how salient each potential stakeholder might be to your company, take the following steps:

a) List potential stakeholders.

b) Rate how the stakeholder is impacted by your company. Do your operations legitimately affect them? What degree of influence do you exert? How intensely? Rank influence, legitimacy, and urgency relative to your company on a scale from 0 to 7.

c) Average those scores (columns $b + d + e$ divided by 3).

d) Now rate how the company is impacted by the stakeholder. To what degree can the stakeholder affect your company? Can they affect your operations? To what degree can they influence you? How intensely and how quickly?

e) Average those scores (columns $f + g + h$ divided by 3).

f) Add the sums of rating from the perspective of the stakeholder and from the perspective of the company $(e + i)$. Divide this sum by 2. This is the stakeholder salience score $0-7$.

Stakeholder salience helps you prioritize which groups you will need to pay most attention to. The salience of stakeholders shifts over time as your business context changes. You should review the salience of your stakeholders frequently. This methodology is one simple way to rank priority.

It is a good idea to get the input of key colleagues in this process. Some companies also factor in the views of key external stakeholders in their analysis. There are other ways to assess scores to the influence and impact of your stakeholders as well. The key point we are making here is that it should be assessed. Scoring methodologies help you through the process and help you communicate stakeholder impact and management both inside and outside your company (Table 2).

Once you have determined the stakeholders' salience score, take a minute to list the issues for which they are seeking attention. Which can you affect with your programs? Are there overlapping concerns? This is where you will need to apply some creativity and judgment about what should and can be done to address the concerns of your stakeholders and thereby make your operating context stronger and more stable. Again, including a group of your key colleagues in this part of the process may help expand scenario planning and provide richer insights (Table 3).

Looking at just the two examples above, you can see that there are some issues on the list of concerns to employees that you cannot probably affect (pay rates) and somewhere you might be able to contribute some solutions. Though the concerns of the community gardeners are low on your priority list, you may be able to engage them in an issue that is of interest to your employees and thereby build some political capital with both groups. Always look for overlapping interests.

KEEP SCANNING THE HORIZON

Although we've talked about the importance of not jumping too fast into the hot issues, you do need to know what's happening on the issues landscape as a whole. McDonalds could never have adapted its corporate citizenship strategies so effectively over time if it had not been aware of what was happening in the media, social, health, and environmental arenas. For instance, in 1995, 75 percent of all media articles about obesity focused on it as an issue of personal responsibility rather than corporate responsibility.

Table 3: Stakeholder Issue Tracker

Salience Rank	Stakeholder	Issues of Concern to Stakeholder	Impact of Stakeholder on Company	Likelihood H/M/L	Severity H/M/L
6.15	Employees	Pay rates	Productivity, turnover cost	H	M
6.15	Employees	Leadership development, learning on the job	Productivity, turnover cost	H	M
6.15	Employees	Quality of community surrounding work site	Productivity, turnover cost	H	M
1.5	Community Garden Association	Horticultural standards in neighborhood planting	Distraction from priority commitments	M	L

Over the next five years this number was completely inverted, with 75 percent of the responsibility being shouldered by food and drink corporations.[5] These articles had a direct and immediate impact on McDonalds' customers, which meant they needed to take action. And they did.

After you have identified your stakeholder groups, make note of the issues that you either know are of concern or suspect might be. You can now begin to map these onto a materiality matrix in the areas that correlate to their ranking. You can move them up or down a bit based on their likelihood and the severity of the issue. Use your judgment. This is art and science and remember that the stakeholders and their issues can and will move over time (Figures 5 and 6).

Figure 5: Materiality Matrix for Issue Management. Use this framework as a way to prioritize the issues that your stakeholders are concerned with and that affect your company. This model provides a way for thinking about how much effort and resource you will allocate to specific issue

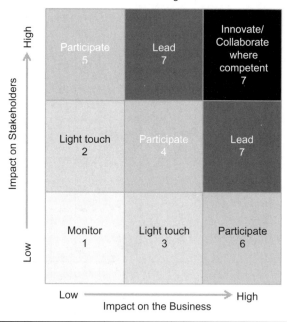

Figure 6: CEMEX Material Issues, Goals Developed in Consultation with Stakeholders

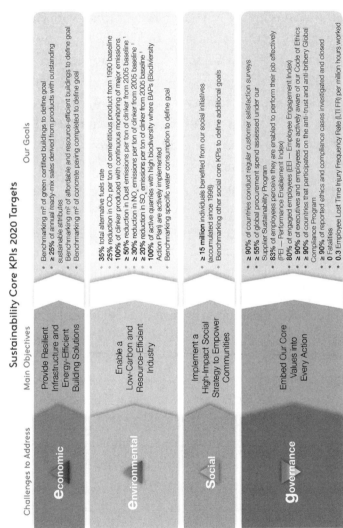

Sustainability Core KPIs 2020 Targets

Challenges to Address | Main Objectives | Our Goals

economic — Provide Resilient Infrastructure and Energy-Efficient Building Solutions
- Benchmarking m² of green certified buildings to define goal
- ≥ 25% of annual ready-mix sales derived from products with outstanding sustainable attributes
- Benchmarking m² of affordable and resource-efficient buildings to define goal
- Benchmarking m² of concrete paving completed to define goal

environmental — Enable a Low-Carbon and Resource-Efficient Industry
- 35% total alternative fuels rate
- 25% reduction in CO_2 per ton of cementitious product from 1990 baseline
- 100% of clinker produced with continuous monitoring of major emissions
- ≥ 50% reduction in Dust emissions per ton of clinker from 2005 baseline [1]
- ≥ 30% reduction in NO_x emissions per ton of clinker from 2005 baseline [1]
- ≥ 20% reduction in SO_x emissions per ton of clinker from 2005 baseline [1]
- 100% of active quarries with high biodiversity where BAP's (Biodiversity Action Plan) are actively implemented
- Benchmarking specific water consumption to define goal

Social — Implement a High-Impact Social Strategy to Empower Communities
- ≥ 15 million individuals benefited from our social initiatives (accumulated since 1998)
- Benchmarking other social core KPIs to define additional goals

governance — Embed Our Core Values into Every Action
- ≥ 90% of countries conduct regular customer satisfaction surveys
- ≥ 55% of global procurement spend assessed under our Supplier Sustainability Program
- 83% of employees perceive they are enabled to perform their job effectively (PEI — Performance Enablement Index)
- 80% of engaged employees (EEI — Employee Engagement Index)
- ≥ 90% of executives and employees are actively aware of our Code of Ethics
- ≥ 90% of countries that participated on the anti-trust and anti-bribery Global Compliance Program
- ≥ 90% of reported ethics and compliance cases investigated and closed
- 0 Fatalities
- 0.3 Employee Lost Time Injury Frequency Rate (LTI FR) per million hours worked

1. Target level of performance to reach every year from 2015-2020

On the left-hand side is your stakeholders' ability to?influence or impact your business, low to high. The X?axis shows your stakeholders' ability to be influenced by or be impacted by your business, low to high. Those in the upper right hand are those you've identified as most important; these are the groups who have a significant relationship with your business *and* who can have a strong impact on your business — they're the ones you should be devoting most of your resources to. If you are able to implement projects that benefit these groups, and they in turn benefit you, you've created a magical win-win scenario. At the highest level of engagement your company will be working with these groups collaboratively and applying your core competence to develop solutions to pressing environmental and social problems. You can also create an incredibly helpful feedback loop. By identifying the right stakeholders you get feedback from a group of ?people who matter to you, so you're able to understand their expectations of your company. You're also more likely to stick with this relationship for a longer period of time. When you work with these people over time and stay focused on issues that affect them long term, your corporate citizenship initiatives are seen as more credible, by this group as well as others in your organization. This improves relationships with your customers, your employees, and your managers. You and your company are seen as authentic.

Don't ignore the people in the lower left-hand quadrant, who you know have both a low likelihood of being impacted by your corporate citizenship program *and* low influence over it. Instead, keep an eye on them and monitor over time. As your company's context changes, they might start to move into the upper right? corner of the quadrant. You don't need to engage with them now, you just need to stay aware.

Notes from the Field

· ·

Stakeholders — A Key Resource in Materiality?Analysis

Martha Patricia Herrera is CEMEX Director of Corporate Social Responsibility and the CEMEX Center for the Development of Sustainable Communities. She also serves as Director of Corporate Affairs in Mexico

At CEMEX we work intensively with stakeholders to determine which issues are most material to the company and its operating environment. Understanding what our priorities are from perspectives in and outside of the company allows us to align our time, resources, and investment accordingly. That's why we have put so much effort into working with our key stakeholders and our Sustainability Advisory Committee to develop the CEMEX Sustainability Materiality Matrix. Through detailed analysis, we have identified the economic, social, environmental, and governance issues that are of greatest concern to both internal and external stakeholders — reinforcing many of our ideas, and bringing fresh perspectives and insights to several issues. Our stakeholders provide input to:

- Identify issues of highest importance to CEMEX and its stakeholders;

- Define risks and opportunities; help set goals and targets;

- Flag areas requiring immediate attention ("urgent" issues);

- Guide sustainability reporting.

Stakeholder engagement is a complex — and sometimes challenging — undertaking. Our local stakeholder partnerships are too numerous to mention. We have several key global relationships that inform much of our work. In addition to the United Nations Environment Program's Sustainable Building and Climate Initiative (SBCI), United Nations Global Compact (UNGC), and World Business Council for Sustainable Development (WBCSD); we count the following among our key global stakeholder relationships:

We have a ten-year agreement with BirdLife International, the largest network of independent conservation organizations in the world. BirdLife works with local communities to promote the sustainable use of natural resources in order to conserve bird habitat — a sentinel indicator of the health of an ecosystem. BirdLife is a leading expert on biodiversity trends across the world. We work with them to implement conservation ?measures at our quarries around the world. We will also ?support wider initiatives to raise awareness of wild birds and biodiversity.

We collaborate with Conservation International to support global biodiversity conservation efforts and raise awareness. We have worked with them to publish several of our conservation books.

We have a partnership with International Union for Conservation of Nature (IUCN) to strengthen our approach to water issues. With more than 1000 government and NGO members and almost 11,000 volunteer scientists in more than 160 countries, IUCN is the world's oldest and largest global environmental network.

We participate in the highest levels of policy debate as a member of the Prince of Wales EU Corporate Leaders Group on Climate Change, which brings together business leaders from a cross-sectoral grouping of international companies who see an urgent need to develop new and longer-term policies to address climate change.

Founded in 1943 by a group of visionary Mexican entrepreneurs, Tec de Monterrey's multidimensional system has grown to include 33 campuses across Mexico, a Virtual University that reaches 23 countries, and several specialized research and knowledge-transfer centers, including its recently launched Institute for Sustainable Social Development.

Our stakeholder relationships have helped us to move forward faster than we might have without them. The work in managing stakeholder programs pays tremendous dividends to CEMEX.

YOUR MOST IMPORTANT STAKEHOLDER GROUP

One final note: the most vital group is your company's employees, and as a result your relationship with the human resources department is key. A huge part of what most corporations want to achieve today is a stable, productive workforce with low turnover, and that's a big challenge. If you're able to offer your HR department corporate citizenship schemes that will help with employee engagement, productivity, and recruitment, and improve the reputation of the company as a positive force in the community, you're going to gain much more enlistment from them than if your program simply focuses on your own needs. You can more effectively recruit employees into your strategy with HR as an ally, and you'll be much better able to measure employee outcomes if you engage with HR because they're the ones who run the annual employee engagement survey. Developing a close and trusting relationship with HR can only bring benefits to both parties.

Another area of similarity between HR and corporate citizenship is that HR is the only other department to manage both soft and hard measures. Soft measures are about engagement with perception, culture, and morale, and hard measures are cost of turnover, recruitment expenses, and productivity results. So approaching them with a mindset that encompasses how you can support both kinds of measures is incredibly important.

WHAT WE'VE COVERED

- Your corporate citizenship program begins and ends with your stakeholders.

- You need to tailor your program to your stakeholders' needs.

- The five main groups of stakeholders are: employees, customers, investors, suppliers, government and environment, and each can affect and be affected by your program.

- Follow your stakeholders, not the issues, but monitor all issues over time.

- Your most important stakeholder group is your employees, thus, your relationship with the HR department is critical.

10 QUESTIONS TO ANSWER BEFORE YOU MOVE ON

1. Have you identified your key stakeholders and do you understand which have the greatest impact on your company and are most important to your corporate citizenship program?

2. Do you understand which stakeholders are most impacted by your company and how your corporate citizenship program could address their concerns?

3. Do you know how your stakeholders interact with each other?

4. Have you created a matrix or mapped out the issues most important to them?

5. What do you want each of these stakeholders to know about your company and what do you want them do to/act on that information?

6. Do you know what your employees care about the most — does it vary by generation or geographic location?

7. How might these issues change over time?

8. What are the inherent risks and opportunities that lie within your stakeholder groups?

9. What timeframe is reasonable to monitor your stakeholder landscape?

10. How are you starting to develop a close relationship with your HR department?

NOTES

1. EPA Sustainability Concepts in Decision-Making: Tools and Approaches for the US Environmental Protection Agency (2012).

2. http://www.nytimes.com/2005/02/20/business/yourmoney/you-want-any-fruit-with-that-big-mac.html?_r=0

3. Bennett and Williams (2011).

4. New York Times (2016, February 2).

5. Lawrence (2004).

4

CONNECTING CORPORATE CITIZENSHIP TO BUSINESS STRATEGY

Strategy without tactics is the slowest route to victory.
Tactics without strategy is the noise before defeat.

SunTzu in *The Art of War*

In the first chapter, you got clear on your business purpose and why it's important. Then you looked outward to your marketplace so you could see how corporate citizenship can create advantage there. The next step is to understand your company's current business strategy so that you can build your corporate citizenship strategy to advance your company's business strategy.

So why is this a big deal? The reason is because your objective is to create both business *and* social value for your company. To do that, you need to understand how your company earns revenue and delivers value to customers and shareholders. Corporate citizenship and business strategy should be closely interwoven to optimize results.

Your first task is to connect your corporate citizenship to your company's business strategy. This has two advantages. First, it will help you make your business case for corporate citizenship internally; second, it will help you to create a plan that really works for the long term, and an agenda that leaders within your business will understand and support. The success you experience as these activities enhance overall business performance will lead to more support. This creates a virtuous cycle that builds upon itself and creates more value for your company and for society.

As a corporate citizenship strategist, the context for your plan is your company, and your company's context is its market, which exists in the broader context of the global economy, our society, and the planet. You have to work through your company to create the impact you want to see in the wider environment, and you do this by understanding your business' priorities, its internal and external stakeholder expectations, and what others in your market are doing. In the same way your corporate citizenship program is not a one size fits all for your employees, neither is it for consumers.

WHAT IS STRATEGY?

The word strategy comes from the Greek word "strategos," which means "army leader." The roots of strategy can be seen in the leadership of ancient empires. In ancient Greece, strategoi were named to lead military arenas and eventually also to govern territorial outposts of the empire. They were elected and made accountable to the citizenry on quantifiable objectives for which they were responsible. The strategoi were almost like the ancient equivalent of corporate vice presidents. Ultimately if they did not perform, they could be removed by the top general (an appointed role that usually went to strategoi who had been successful — not unlike our contemporary CEOs) or by a group of individuals that had an oversight responsibility and who operated, in many ways, like a modern day corporate board.

As it was in ancient times, strategy today is as much about deciding what not to do as it is about deciding what to do. It's all about making decisions on how to mobilize your resources to get results. Carroll School of Management Dean Andy Boynton teaches his top-rated Boston College students that in order to be able to mobilize your forces, strategy has to be:

- *Action oriented*: it describes *what* to do and *why*.

- *Tangible*: it outlines *who* will execute which actions, *the sequence of engagement*, and *how* to measure progress.

- *Important*: it explains *why* you're pursuing one course of action over another, and *what* will be gained and sacrificed.

- *Clear*: it makes your objectives easy to understand. You should be able to explain to a fourth grader *what* is to be done and *why*.

- *Energizing*: your strategy should create a vivid image of success for your team. What does it *look like*? This is a point even great strategists often leave out.

A strategy is an integrated, over-arching, clearly communicated concept of how objectives will be achieved. Tactics, on the other hand, comprise a detailed plan of separate actions that are designed to put the strategy into practice.

WHAT IS A CORPORATE BUSINESS STRATEGY?

There are almost as many definitions of strategy as there are business strategies. We describe strategy as a plan of action designed to achieve an objective. Ultimately it comprises a set of goals, combined with a plan for how to differentiate the company among competitors and use the company's resources in the best possible way to achieve those desired outcomes.

There are many great strategy books available. No matter what strategy framework you are using to analyze your arena of engagement, you'll be examining at least five core aspects of your plan to compete.

Economic Logic

Your economic logic is defined by understanding how your firm makes money. Are you low-cost in your product category through scope or scale? Premium price and service? Premium price due to proprietary features? How much of the value of your product is in its brand and reputation? Is your product easily replicated (commodity?), mostly similar but customized to some extent? Or crafted individually for each customer?

Competitors

The more customers you have the more likely it is your competitors will want to earn some of your business. These companies comprise not only current competitors but also up and comers. If your business has low barriers to entry (in other words, you don't need much human or financial capital or technological expertise to get started), competition will likely be steeper. Often there are others who can provide the products and services your customers buy from you; the more substitutes exist, the more bargaining power customers have.

Customers

If your company has a lot of customers, that's a good thing. However, a large market will also attract more competitors. Understanding who your actual customers are can be tricky. For example, you may think of Campbell Soup Company as a consumer company, but Campbell actually sells its products to the retailers who distribute the product, not directly to individual consumers. Understanding all of your firm's customer relationships is very important.

Supply Chain

The fewer suppliers you buy from the more reliant you are on them, and their bargaining power increases. Try thinking about the people and resources needed to run your business as the "ingredients" in the recipe for success. Each company needs similar types of ingredients (materials, labor, etc.), but depending on the industry they require these ingredients in vastly different proportions and prepared in different ways. Companies spend a significant amount of effort on eliminating risk and building resilience across supply chains.

Market Arena

Where are we active and with how much emphasis? Which geographic regions? What are our product categories and market segments? What are our product platforms and technologies? Understanding where we want to compete, both in geography and in category, is critical to maintaining discipline around where we will expend resources and where we will not.

YOUR OWN COMPANY'S STRATEGY

Take a moment to understand the strategy of the corporation you work for by answering the questions in Table 4. You might not know all the answers yet, but the exercise will help you identify the gaps in your knowledge. We have met many corporate citizenship professionals who have a very clear view of what programs they want to implement, but have a very difficult time describing them within the context of their company's strategy or competitive environment. Trust us when we say that developing this level of business acumen is critical to achieving your goals.

Take a minute to fill out Table 4. First, answer all of the questions about your company's business strategy to the best of your ability. Once you have completed the top row of questions, take a few minutes to think about how your corporate citizenship program can help achieve those business objectives. Does your company seek to attract top talent in a technical area? Employee involvement programs and matching gifts might help. Does your product require materials or ingredients that could be sustainably sourced? Working with an industry association on sustainably sourced goods or codes of conduct for producers may be a program you should undertake. Use this canvas to look for the intersections of your business strategy and corporate citizenship program. This is where you can find the greatest value for your company and for society.

Table 4: Business Strategy Worksheet

Business Strategy Questions

Customers	Supply Chain	Economic Logic	Market Arenas	Competitors
Who are your company's key customers? What do you know about them? What problem might you solve for them? What do they care about? Are they driven by cost? Quality? Customization? Convenience? Differentiation? Are they individuals or other companies or both? Where are they located? What can you offer that no other company can?	What does your company need to run its business? Who are its suppliers? Do they have raw materials to Manage? Are there human rights or environmental risks in the supply chain? Do they need highly skilled employees to deliver products or services? Will they be in competition for employees, technology, or other inputs? What are the "ingredients" of the company's success?	How does the company make money? Low-cost in product category through scope or scale? Margin versus growth? Premium price and service? Premium price due to proprietary features? How much of the value of product is in its brand equity? Is product easily replicated (commodity?), mostly similar but customized to some extent? Or crafted individually for each customer?	Is your company looking to new geographic regions, acquisitions/ partners or products for growth? Who is there already or positioned to get there before you? What do they do that you could adapt to improve your performance? Are there capabilities that you possess that would be valuable to other markets? Against what companies are you compared either in or beyond your industry?	What are other companies in the industry and sector doing? What do they do better? Who provides an alternative for the product(s) or service(s)? What do you offer that others do not? Which aspects of the business need to be reinforced to ensure competitive differentiation? What areas could be strengthened? What would it take for that to happen?

How can corporate citizenship add value?				
How can you support your customers' values? What issues are they involved with? Do your B2B customers have corporate citizenship objectives? How can you support them? How can corporate citizenship add value?	What environmental and social issues must be addressed to maintain necessary supplies? Codes of conduct? Environmental or social issue management programs? How can corporate citizenship add value?	Are there environmental or social issues that must be Addressed to sustain your economic model or deliver competitive advantage? Which stakeholders Influence your success? How can corporate citizenship add value?	Which locations? Which people? Which issues do we need to play to support our business purpose and goals? Our social objectives? How can corporate citizenship add value?	What are other companies doing? In your sector? Beyond your industry and sector? How can you bring innovation or creativity to your company? Can you help to ensure that your company is differentiated? How can corporate citizenship add value?

HOW DO YOU FIND OUT ABOUT YOUR COMPANY'S STRATEGY?

While completing this exercise, you may have realized how little you know about your own company's over-arching strategy. This isn't unusual, nor is it uncommon to be unsure about how to find out more. If you're like many corporate professionals, you'll find these policies tend to get communicated down from the top. The further down the chain of command you are, the less information you may receive about strategy. In fact, most people in large companies know less about their company's strategy than you will after working through this chapter.

If your company culture isn't one in which strategy is discussed openly, one way to find out about it is to read your company website; it probably won't explicitly say what the strategy is, but it will certainly signal it. Specifically, the "mission and purpose" section of the site (often found on its "About" page), and the investor relations section with the Securities and Exchange Commission (SEC) filings and transcriptions of analyst calls, will help you find out what your company sees as its major areas of risk and opportunity. Read the risk and disclosure sections of your company's 10K SEC filing; many corporations include ESG risks that your corporate citizenship strategy can affect positively.

Do this bit of research now before you move on; it will help you when you come to create your own corporate citizenship strategy. As you're doing this, make a note of the risks and opportunities in each of the five dimensions of your business strategy:

- Competitors
- Market arena
- Economic logic
- Customers
- Supply chain

In each of these, there are six broad categories of stakeholders that can affect your company's ability to execute its strategy:

- Employees

- Investors

- Customers

- Suppliers

- Governments

- Environment

As you read through your notes on your company's business strategy, jot down to the right of each of your answer boxes which of the stakeholders above are most critical to your firm's ability to execute its strategy. Is there one which emerges as more prominent than the others? This is an indication of how you might focus your program.

CONNECTING YOUR CORPORATE CITIZENSHIP TO YOUR BUSINESS STRATEGY

How does your company intend to "win"? For instance, if it has a global growth plan your social investment should not be entirely domestic. Or if your corporation intends to recruit large numbers of new staff, your programs should focus on how you're going to connect with these new employees. Does the intersection of technology play a major role in your business strategy and if so, how can you leverage that? Or if a large portion of your government business is based on military contracts (e.g., health care benefit business), you want a sizeable presence within the government military sector. Conversely, companies generally should not engage in a cause du jour, for example, if you have a limited connection to military customers or employees, don't engage in military/veteran programs.

WHICH ASSETS ARE MOST IMPORTANT?

Nobody wants to lose the value they've built in any of their business assets or stakeholder relationships. Remember, however, that strategy is choice and you can't do everything. You'll have to prioritize how you allocate your budgets and what you do first, second, third, and so on.

While we talk about your corporate citizenship strategy, remember your corporate citizenship program is a set of tactics that advances your overall business strategy. So now let's get more specific about how your corporate citizenship can support your business objectives.

Corporate citizenship programs return value to companies in specific ways, and one size doesn't fit all. Take a minute to look at Table 5. If you read it from left to right you can see each resource is most effectively leveraged by different types of programs. Table 5 is useful because it helps to focus on which types of corporate citizenship tactics are best aligned to affect the advantage you are seeking for your company and the change you would like to make in the world. When you understand the mechanisms of value-creation you can use your resources more effectively to achieve the results you want.

For example, if your company strategy relies on being able to recruit and retain a highly skilled workforce, you should be thinking about developing programs that affect employees — recruitment, training and development, labor practices, philanthropy, employee volunteering, sustainability, and reporting. You can see the programs most effective at influencing employees are different than those you might need to use if, for instance, you're highly dependent on natural resources. Of course there's some overlap, and many companies will develop a portfolio of activities across many of these program types.

Take a minute now to circle the activities you think will be most important to your company, based on your business strategy. Is there one that seems more important than the others? Put a star next to that circle (Table 5).

Understanding Table 5 is an important part of your work. Because strategy is choice about what you will and will not do, it is critically important to understand HOW corporate citizenship can create value for your business. When you understand the mechanisms of value-creation, you can more effectively deploy resources to yield the results that you seek efficiently.

ISSUE FOCUS

Deciding which issues you will try to address with your corporate citizenship program is one of the most important decisions you will make. In addition to thinking about aspects of your business strategy that you can support, there are issues in your operating context that are impacted by your company and that your company can be affected by. These issues can take the form of risks or opportunities.

As we discussed in Chapter 2, a key responsibility of the corporate citizenship strategist is to continue to scan the horizon to monitor your context and identify emerging (and waning) opportunities and risks. Use the space above to list the issues that you identified in that chapter in Table 2. Which of these can affect your company's ability to pursue its strategy? Do these issues mostly represent opportunities or threats? Mark each with a "T" or an "O".

Let's start with the risks or threats to your company. Ask yourself, where is my company's operating context most likely to be affected? If the likelihood that your company will be affected is high, put a mark toward the right of the likelihood axis (Figure 7).

Now ask yourself how severely would your company be affected if the risk you have identified was realized. Look at where those marks intersect and jot down the issue in that position on the matrix.

The issues that are in the red zone are your priority risk management issues. These are issues that your corporate citizenship

Table 5: Logic Models for How Corporate Citizenship Creates Business Value

Stakeholder	Effective Activities	Impact on Group	Outcomes	Value of Company	Contingencies
Employees	Sustainability	New skills and training	Eased recruitment and lower turnover	Decreased costs	Industry
	Labor practices	Recruitment and retention	Better teamwork and higher productivity; improved performance	Increased revenue	Employee tenure/experience
	Philanthropy	Increased engagement			Company size
	Employee volunteering				
	Sustainability				Perceived authenticity
Customers	Cause branding	Higher loyalty	Repurchase and higher share of category spending	Increased market value	Substitutes
	Philanthropy	Favorable reputation	Referrals and willingness to pay premium	Increased revenue	Industry
	Sustainability	Higher satisfaction			Quality of product or service
	Innovation and design	Higher purchase intent			Perception of CSR premium
	Cause marketing				View of authenticity substitutes
Investors	Sustainability	Improved reputation	Lower cost of capital	Decreased costs	Volume of institutional or SRI investors
	Innovation and design	Decreased long-term risk profile	Increased stock valuations	Increased revenue	
	Supply chain management	Expanded product portfolio			
	Disclosure				
	Governance				

Stakeholder / Activity				
Suppliers				
Training programs	Reduce waste	New supplier capability	Reduced cost of production	Scale
Extend ESG standards to suppliers	Lower risk	Share risk across industry where you cannot differentiate	Increase revenue	Competition for resource
Disclosure requirements	Secure materials and labor predictably	Develop product premium (e.g., fair trade product)	Improved forecast ability	Differentiation of resource
Codes of conduct/standards	New supplier capability			
Government				
Environmental	Develop connections to decision-makers	Reduced lobbying cost	Decreased cost	Maturity of government
Community involvement	Shape policies and regulatory environment	Access to government purchasing	Increased revenue	Degree of bureaucracy
Voluntary standards	License to operate			
	Develop consensus standard of operation			
Environment				
Pollution reductions	Reduce waste	Alternative materials	Reduce cost of production	Cost of alternatives
Natural resource conservation	Lower risk	Share risk across industry where you cannot differentiate	Increase revenue	Competition for resource
Sustainable alternatives	Secure materials predictably	Develop product premium (e.g., fair trade product)	Improved forecast ability	Differentiation of resource
Codes of conduct/standards	Supply resilience			

Figure 7: Issue Tracking

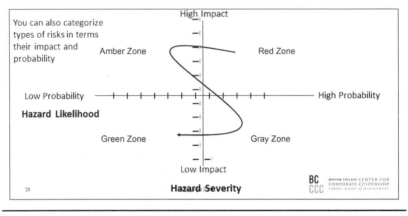

program should address to improve your risk profile and improve your operating context. The amber zone should be closely monitored and as issues become more probable you should begin program development. Issues in the gray and green zones should be continually monitored for increased probability and impact.

Now let's look at your opportunities. Are there opportunities that your company is especially well-positioned to be able to take advantage of? Can you see places where your corporate citizenship program can support the business strategy and create greater strength where there is an opportunity in order to create greater competitive advantage? Can you help your company mobilize against a threat? Competition for employees, for example, can be improved with employee volunteer programs, employee campaigns, innovative work arrangements and benefits, leadership development programs, etc. All of these can be enhanced through corporate citizenship programs.

Take a minute to look back at your business strategy on page 74–75 and list your strengths and weaknesses down the left side in Figure 8. These are internally controlled. You and others in your company prioritize efforts and investment to maintain and develop strengths and mitigate weaknesses.

Now list your opportunities and threats across the top in Figure 8. These are forces that are exerted on your business from outside of your operations. Think not only about how you can improve your operating context to be better able to address your business strategy but also ask whether there are social or environmental issues that your company is uniquely positioned to help address. Opportunities and threats are controlled largely by external forces. You need to be monitoring them constantly in order to be able to prioritize which investments you should make to maximize your competitive advantage (Figure 8).

Figure 8 is a sample SWOT analysis format for you to use. List your strengths and weaknesses down the left side and your opportunities and threats across the top. Now look at where your strengths can either help you achieve an opportunity or

Figure 8: SWOT Analysis Form

		Opportunities						Threats						
	SWOT Analysis Form	Large # of well-trained grads in new market						Competition for recruits						
Strengths	Strong recruiting department	X						X						
Weaknesses	Low engagement for freshman employees							X						

avoid a threat. If a particular strength is able to do either, put an "X" in the box where they intersect. Look at your weaknesses and do the same thing. Mark an "X" where your weaknesses may prevent you from taking advantage of an opportunity or make you vulnerable to a threat (Figure 9).

COMPETITIVE ADVANTAGE

Where you have strengths that can help you take advantage of opportunities, you have competitive advantage. The more Xs you have in the boxes, the stronger your competitive advantage (Figure 9). This advantage should be preserved and strengthened if possible. Are there dimensions of your corporate citizenship program that can help? Refer to Table 5 to help you think about what types of programs are best suited to enhance the assets that you need most and address the issues that represent the biggest risks and opportunities for your company. Remember, you can

Figure 9: SWOT Analysis Quadrants

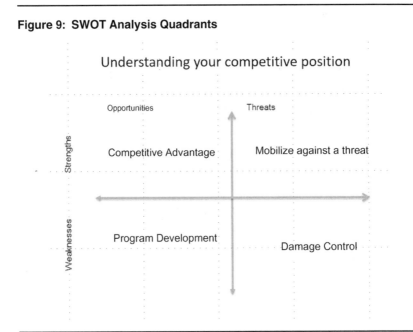

increase competitive advantage by reducing weaknesses or eliminating threats. It's not all about the size of the box (after all, there are more opportunities in the world than you could ever pursue). The purpose of this exercise is to get you to think hard about which opportunities you are well-positioned to pursue and which will require significant additional investments.

Sidebar 1: FedEx and EMBARQ

CONNECTING STRENGTH TO OPPORTUNITY

FedEx is admired widely for its logistical and transportation expertise. The company seeks to work with organizations that can benefit from those capabilities. When FedEx executives spoke with the leaders at EMBARQ, the Center for Sustainable Transport at the World Resources Institute, they knew they had found the right fit. EMBARQ works in cities around the globe because 75 percent of global CO_2 emissions come from cities, and the greatest challenge in addressing that problem is a significant lack of sustainable transportation. FedEx and EMBARQ are now working together on solutions to a problem that will only get worse as urban populations continue to grow. FedEx provides assistance on a number of advisory projects for EMBARQ, including a leadership development program for EMBARQ staff held at FedEx headquarters in Memphis, TN. The program helps EMBARQ staff build sustainable public transport and make informed decisions about which buses to purchase for the most fuel-efficient, safe transportation networks. The collaboration between EMBARQ and FedEx is also providing high-quality training to city bus drivers in Mexico City and Guadalajara. Road safety and congestion are significant issues for logistics companies and this partnership not only addresses important social (transportation) and environmental (CO emissions) issues, it also helps to improve the operating context for a company that operates in almost every city in the world.

PROGRAM DEVELOPMENT

Where you have weaknesses that intersect with opportunities you have the opportunity for program development. As you convert weaknesses to strengths, your competitive advantage quadrant will get larger. That is a good thing! Again, remember that part of this exercise is about prioritizing. One way to understand the level of priority that should be placed on improving a weakness is to look at how many opportunities and threats could be addressed by improving that capability. If only one or two issues (opportunities or risks) among a long list of possibilities could be affected, this is probably not a good investment.

Sidebar 2: Brown-Forman Industry Leadership

ADDRESSING A THREAT WITH STRENGTH

Moderating consumption of food and alcohol were broadly considered the responsibility of the individual 10 years ago. Public opinion has shifted over time and now companies are expected to help consumers make good choices about their personal behavior.

Brown-Forman, one of the top 10 global spirit companies, strikes a balance between marketing to sell products and promoting the responsible use of its products. The company can count among its accomplishments great brand stories, growing market share, and increasing sales. At the same time, they understand that unmodulated promotion can shatter the trust necessary to win customer loyalty. One way the company navigates this potential pitfall is by integrating corporate citizenship into their marketing, leveraging its brand to influence consumer behavior, and encourage better personal choices, which translates into social benefits that reinforce the brand. The company sponsors wide-ranging efforts of various organizations to prevent alcohol abuse. The promotion of each brand integrates a message that balances enjoyment with responsible use — one example being Southern Comfort's "Start and end things right: Drink responsibly."

Employees at Brown-Forman, called "ambassadors of responsibility," are expected to lead by example. Reinforcing this expectation are global employee training programs on alcohol responsibility, company events, and wellness efforts. In 2009, Brown-Forman developed a board game, "Think and Drink Tavern," to supplement employee education on responsible drinking. Teams compete against each other, drawing cards that test their knowledge and facilitate discussions about handling real-life situations, at company events and in their personal lives, involving alcohol. All new hires (domestic and international) participate in the game during weeklong global orientations, at company headquarters in Louisville, KY.

This leadership extends to the broader industry as Brown-Forman led CEOs of competitor companies in developing collective commitments to strengthen efforts to prevent harmful use of alcohol. This collaboration with other members of the Global Alcohol Producers Group targets 10 actions over a five-year period to reduce underage drinking.

Brown-Forman used its considerable marketing and communications strength to address an issue that is threatening to its industry.

DAMAGE CONTROL

We hope your damage control quadrant is very small. If you have a significant number of weaknesses that make you vulnerable to a significant number of threats in your operating context, you want to mitigate these as soon as possible. Especially if the threats are in the red or amber categories — meaning that their impact could be significant and their likelihood is great.

MOBILIZE AGAINST A THREAT

If you have a strength that can mitigate a threat before it becomes a significant issue for damage control, you want to do that. Because you have capability in that area already, this does not usually require additional investment, so it is important to prioritize whether the capability is better applied to a potential advantage or to managing a risk. How severe is the hazard of the risk to your company?

PRESENTING YOUR WORK

You have done most of the analysis that you need to do to get started. Here is a format to start organizing the work that you've done thus far.

Executive Summary

This is where you summarize the main points of your strategy, including the timescales, costs, and main activities you're proposing. It's not to be confused with an introduction; it should give the reader a summary, in a paragraph or two, of your whole document. Though it is typically presented first in the document, it should be written last.

Situational Analysis

This is where you will summarize your SWOT analysis.

As part of this section, highlight key issues you have identified in your situational analysis. This will help you create a plan that solves problems as well as takes advantage of opportunities.

Objectives

This is a short section listing both short- and long-term objectives. Which internal and external issues do you intend to address with your strategy? What is your rationale for selecting these issues? Where will your programs add value for your business and for society? What do you intend to accomplish?

Strategic Plan

What will you do? What activities do you intend to carry out and how will they deliver on what you intend to accomplish? When will you do these activities and in what order? How does the plan exploit key resources? How does it reinforce important elements of your company's culture? Are the elements of your strategy differentiated or do they represent a "me-too" approach?

There are five criteria against which you can measure your program to determine whether you are really delivering maximum value to your company and to society:

Criterion 1: Your corporate citizenship efforts are maximized against what other corporations are doing. Successful strategies of others are adopted and improved.

Criterion 2: Causes supported *and issue foci* connect logically to the core competence of the company and its business context.

Criterion 3: The causes supported are important to your communities of operation or customers. They are relevant to maintaining your assets.

Criterion 4: You are reinforcing your points of corporate differentiation.

Criterion 5: Corporate citizenship investments achieve the impacts sought — both in the business and with causes supported. You know because you measure.

Budgets

What will it cost to carry out your plan of action? Do you have the financial and human resources to get the work done? If not, how will you get them?

DON'T FORGET THE "BECAUSE"

What is the logic behind your strategy? How will you actually measure success? Do you have the resources, financial and intellectual, to be able to measure impact? Or can you only go as far as outputs? Only around 20 percent of companies measure impact of their corporate citizenship programs, and even then on only 20 percent of their programs.[1] To do this often requires expertise and involvement from other people, and sometimes from people outside the company (Figure 10). What is your company's appetite to measure impact?

Figure 10: Logic Models — Begin with the End in Mind. This figure can help you think about what your measure of success will be and how you will describe them as you present your corporate citizenship strategy

Input	Activities	Outputs	Outcomes	Impacts
Resources dedicated to or consumed by the project	What the project does with its inputs to achieve its mission	The volume of work accomplished by a project	Benefits or changes for participants during and after the project	Long term consequences of the intervention
Usually a noun	Usually a gerund, ends in -ing	Usually a quantity	Usually a change	A fundamental change in a system or society
Planned Work		Intended Results		

BC
CCC   BOSTON COLLEGE CENTER FOR
      CORPORATE CITIZENSHIP

Depending on your capabilities, you may not be able to measure all impacts or even outcomes. Take a project to clean up a local river-bed, for example. You can count the hours of volunteer time and weigh the tons of trash removed, but the long-term benefits such as water quality, or fishery resilience, may be impossible to quantify without a longitudinal study and a huge research budget. Understanding up front whether there is an appetite for this kind of investment should inform the level of granularity in your measurement.

One simple way to challenge yourself and your team on impacts and outcomes is to leverage the "why?" exercise. When you propose an activity or program for which you find it difficult to measure impact, ask yourself why you're doing the particular activity or program. In the river clean-up example noted above, you may believe the "why" is to build stronger teamwork and provide employees with a better sense of your community. Then ask yourself *why* that is important. Perhaps you believe the employees will have a better perception of your company through the service or participate more in employee giving programs (guess what — both of these outcomes can be measured if you do the baseline measurements up front). Perhaps you believe that employees that engage in community service are more productive and contribute more in the workplace. Talk to your HR team — they may have a way to test that impact measure, for instance engagement scores on annual employee surveys. Keep asking yourself *why* and you'll often get to a measurable impact!

If your company is ready to make a long-term commitment to improve a specific social or environmental cause, you can design for measurement. For instance, if you're setting up a partnership with an NGO, you can specify that a condition of funding would be for the NGO to provide specific data so that you can measure impacts and outcomes.

One key planning consideration is measurement at the beginning of a project, not at the end. Far too many corporate citizenship professionals consider measurement after a project or initiative was successful — then come to realize they needed to measure a baseline or starting point to show impact.

MAKE SURE YOU'VE COVERED ALL YOUR BASES

Once you go through the exercise of writing your strategy, if your company competes by providing superior service, for example, you'll want to make sure you are an employer of choice (making recruitment easier), and that the employees who provide that service are knowledgeable about your offerings and fully engaged on behalf of the company (and therefore likely to stay longer and provide better service to customers). In this case, an element of your corporate citizenship program should focus on employee volunteer programs that provide opportunities for leadership development and mentoring. If you're in a resource-intensive industry, you may want to focus more on environmental sustainability and natural resource stewardship and engage employees in the topic in a variety of ways including "green teams" or resource stewardship councils. If you work in a financial services company, you may want to lead social investment or financial literacy programs. Ask yourself, how can my corporate citizenship connect to top line growth? How does it connect to bottom line savings? How does it mitigate risk?

Does your corporate citizenship strategy fit with your firm's purpose, culture, and corporate strategy?

Do your programs allow everyone at the firm to participate? Who are the leaders of your initiative? Whose patronage do you need to secure for your strategy to be successful? What traditions does your company have that can either be adapted or that must be continued? If you introduced the program tomorrow, do you think most employees would think, "Huh?!" or would they have an immediate reaction of, "Of course!"?

Does your corporate citizenship strategy exploit your key resources and capabilities?

For example, Brown-Forman (one of the largest spirit and wine companies in the United States) is a company that uses a lot of water to produce its product and that sources and grows many commodity ingredients such as corn, sugar, and agave. This company would be better suited to focus on soil and water conservation programs than would Microsoft, which would be well suited to working on programs aimed at increasing access to technology.

Is your corporate citizenship strategy differentiated or does it have a "me-too" approach?

Most corporate citizenship programs will comprise a portfolio of activities that cover a range of topics and almost all will have some programs that are not differentiated. Think of the federated giving campaigns (United Way) as an example. Unless you are the largest giver, there are few ways for the company to be differentiated, though it is often a community expectation that your company participate. The key in these programs is to derive business value out of the effort by building great employee engagement or learning into your specific process. The ultimate goal is to ensure that most elements of your program are differentiated for your company. There are five criteria you can use to judge this:

1. You adopt, and then improve upon what other companies are doing.

2. The causes you support and the issues you focus on connect logically to your company's core competencies.

3. The causes you support are important to your corporation's employees, community, or customers.

4. You're reinforcing your company's points of difference.

5. You measure the impact of your investments so you can see if you've achieved what you set out to accomplish.

Do you have enough resources to pursue your strategy?

You may find that you have many strategic opportunities with your corporate citizenship program, but you don't have sufficient resources to pursue all (or sometimes any) of them fully. Here's where you have to exercise "generalship" and make decisions about which aspects of your potential strategy are most important to pursue. You can also explore alternative ways to execute your program. Can you deliver an independent signature program, or are there opportunities to reduce costs by working in partnerships? Can you run a smaller pilot program that can be scaled up later?

Can you easily communicate your strategy and describe the value it will deliver (again, and again, and again, and again …)?

You should be able to write a brief statement about what value your citizenship program will deliver to your company and society, and why your company is uniquely qualified to deliver that value. It should be simple enough that anyone can understand what you are trying to accomplish. Being repeatable is important, because the average person needs to hear something 3–5 times in order to be able to recall it (never mind act on it).

By answering the questions below, you'll be well on your way to creating a sound corporate citizenship strategy.

WHAT WE'VE COVERED

- Integrating your corporate citizenship strategy with the over-arching business strategy is essential for your plans to be accepted, respected, and effective.

- For this reason, take some time to learn about your business' strategy before you dive into creating your corporate citizenship strategy.

- Now write your own strategy, integrating it into the business strategy.

10 QUESTIONS TO ANSWER BEFORE YOU MOVE ON

1. Can you define what a strategy is (and what it isn't)?

2. What's your company's over-arching business strategy? Do you know how your firm makes money and where? Do you know how your company is differentiated from competitors? Can you identify key issues of concern to customers? In your supply chain?

3. Have you identified issues that are important to your company's success? Have you identified ways your corporate citizenship strategy supports the corporate strategy?

4. What does the future look like if your strategy is successful? How can your corporate citizenship program strengthen your company's strategic position?

5. What will you need to do to get there? Can you engage employees more deeply, address the concerns of investors or customers? Create more sustainable and stable supply chains?

6. Have you written your strategy in such a way that all stakeholders can understand it?

7. Do you have the resources to execute your strategy? If not, what choices will you make about what you will do first and what you will not do? What outcomes will be sacrificed as a result?

8. What are the "table stakes" programs that you will have to do because they are expected of everyone?

9. What will your program accomplish for the company that is different than what competitors are doing?

10. How will you measure success? Do you have the resources to measure the impacts you intend?

NOTE

1. The Boston College Center for Corporate Citizenship (2015).

5

HOW TO SET UP AND ORGANIZE YOUR CORPORATE CITIZENSHIP PROGRAM

Unless you're one of the fortunate few with 20 or 30 people on your corporate citizenship program team (wouldn't that be great?), you'll probably be leading a team of five direct reports or fewer. Perhaps, like many, you're a one-person department seeking to influence a large and diverse company. Even with a lean team, as long as you think carefully about how you use your social influence to mobilize people, you can drive change and generate important results. This chapter is about how to make the most efficient use of your resources to do just that.

THE IMPORTANCE OF NETWORKS AND INFLUENCE

So far we've talked quite a lot about how you start to create influence as a corporate citizenship expert within your organization. If you're knowledgeable about your company's purpose, goals, strategy, and processes, and your corporate citizenship strategy integrates with that of the business, you're three quarters of the way there. Your next step is to figure out who can help you advance the environmental and social investments that will differentiate your company in a successful way.

Connecting your corporate citizenship strategy to business imperatives gives you a roadmap for how to build your network of influence. This is accomplished best by identifying the people who have a vested interest in achieving your objectives. For example, are you responsible for managing your company's disaster relief efforts? If so you'll need to check in with logistics, HR, and communications. Are you working on your company's sustainability report? You should talk to people in many different operational units. Have you identified employee engagement as a citizenship business objective? Then someone in HR should be one of your first connections. Do you think you can reduce your water impact? Connect with your environment department, health and safety team, engineering group, and operations colleagues to get their buy-in and help. Is there a reputation or brand-building opportunity for you? Work with your communications and marketing team. You may not be leading an army, but you can mobilize one by connecting your objectives to their definitions of success. Building an engaged and motivated network will be absolutely fundamental to the success of your program.

These two diagrams (Figure 11) illustrate the interconnectedness of all areas of your business when it comes to implementing and experiencing your corporate citizenship program. The first uses the example of a disaster relief effort, and the second shows the network you need to build in order to implement measurement and report effectively.

The diagrams above illustrate how a single network structure can support two very different activities (sometimes simultaneously). If you have a strong network structure, you have a flexible and resilient team.

The reason networks are so successful is because each part builds on the strengths of the other; being flexible, they give an organization the stability it requires.

So it's clear when you're working out how to execute your corporate citizenship program that you have to think in a networked way. This is commonly referred to as "systems thinking." There

Figure 11: Activating Nodes in Your Professional Network

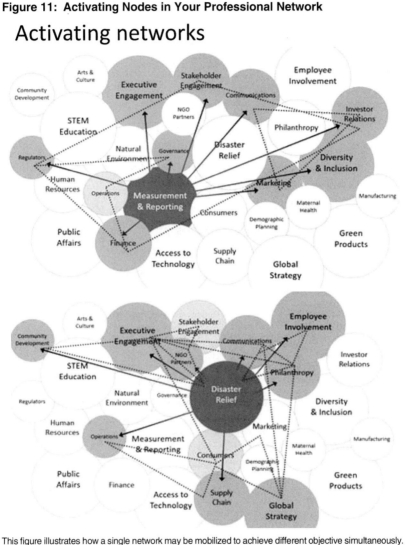

This figure illustrates how a single network may be mobilized to achieve different objective simultaneously.

are five points you'll need to touch, all of which link to each other:

- *Strategy*: your plan for competing.

- *People*: getting the right group together to do the work.

- *Structure*: organizing the team.

- *Processes*: communicating, making decisions, accomplishing the tasks, measuring progress.

- *Metrics and incentives*: keeping people motivated to produce results.

If you make changes to one of these areas it has implications for all, so you always have to be thinking about whether you've organized things so you can achieve what you want.

In his book *Designing Dynamic Organizations*, Jay R. Galbraith created *The Star Model(TM)* to visualize how this works. For Galbraith, a strategy is basically a company's formula for success, encompassing the organization's mission as well as its business goals. Its purpose is to create competitive advantage, and to do that a company has to have superior organizational capabilities. The Galbraith Star Model™ highlights the multiple dimensions of successful strategy implementation (Figure 12). Galbraith's model reminds us that it is not only about formal structures. It is about getting the right people involved, with the right incentives and processes to support the desired outcome. You can develop a Star Model for every program you have to ensure that you have a comprehensive plan that will yield the performance (what we have achieved) and culture (how you have achieved it) you are seeking.

THE RIGHT STRATEGY

We covered strategy and why it's so fundamental to your success in the last chapter, so we won't go into it again here in detail. But it's important to remember that without the right strategy your corporate citizenship program is unlikely to succeed short term, and certainly won't be sustainable in the years to come.

As an example of how this has played out in our own experience comes in Dave's experience as Vice President of Corporate Responsibility and Chief Sustainability Officer of Campbell Soup

Figure 12: The Galbraith Star Model — Organizing for Success

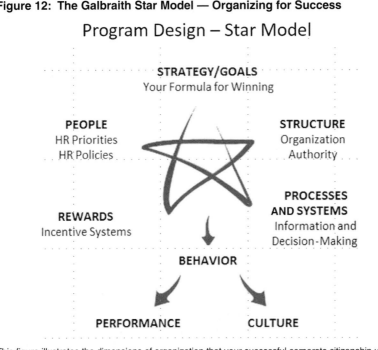

Program Design – Star Model

STRATEGY/GOALS
Your Formula for Winning

PEOPLE
HR Priorities
HR Policies

STRUCTURE
Organization
Authority

PROCESSES
AND SYSTEMS
Information and
Decision-Making

REWARDS
Incentive Systems

BEHAVIOR

PERFORMANCE   CULTURE

This figure illustrates the dimensions of organization that your successful corporate citizenship under-taking should address.
Reproduced from *Designing Organizations* by Jay R. Galbraith. With permission from Jossey-Bass: San Francisco, CA, 2002.

Company. When he first arrived, he was asked to create a situational assessment and full strategic plan within three months, all without a team in place. He had a strong leader and a CEO who wanted a set of demanding goals; he also had a personal view of what success looked like, but knew from previous experience that it would take efforts from every part of the business to achieve it. The challenge he faced initially was bringing the executive team up to speed very quickly on the external environment, competitive landscape, and differentiating strategies he wanted the entire business to embrace — across the existing business divisions from healthy beverages to simple meals and baked snacks and biscuits.

Understandably, the business presidents and functional leaders saw their consumer promise and bottom line priorities through different lenses; brands were delivering on specific consumer promises and internal functions had long-standing operational frameworks. Dave was hired to create a differentiating enterprise-wide strategy that brought together and leveraged strengths across these functions.

Having worked through complex global corporate citizenship challenges in the past, Dave was in a position to help bring in a broader perspective on outside issues with a much longer-term view. The CEO at the time, Doug Conant, proposed setting goals quickly and moving ahead. Dave knew that to drive real change, he needed to build consensus and a sense of ownership among the leadership team. So he went to those business leaders and brand managers and asked how he could help make them more successful long term. The answer was to translate what had to happen within each business unit and for each brand to make it the most competitive in the minds and hearts of consumers. Today's food landscape continues to evolve to reflect consumer values toward transparency and real food.

The value that the team at Campbell sought to bring was a longer term guidance for how those brands and the full enterprise could prepare to be positioned in the same place as consumers were headed. The Campbell team built a strategy that integrated key business drivers and sought to prepare for the future. Campbell's purpose and enterprise strategic plan now clearly reflects Real Food, Transparency and Sustainability as a core strategic imperative.

This is a tangible example of how a corporate citizenship strategy can work in tandem with other company leaders to have a long-term, positive and proactive effect on a brand and the parent company.

THE RIGHT PEOPLE

Getting the right people in your company on board is essential for the success of your strategy implementation. To start this process, you need to work out what your professional network is across the company, where the main corporate citizenship action will take place, and who might be best positioned to help you take action.

Here are the roles you should be considering when you're creating your network:

- The people you want on your teams to do the work.

- Ambassadors for specific campaigns, such as corporate giving or green team initiatives. These people will help you spread the word.

- Project sponsors who have the authority or influence to deploy resources, and who care enough about what you're trying to achieve to use some of their financial or social capital to help you get it done.

Once you've identified your people, how do you go about recruiting them? The best way is to invite them to participate, and when someone raises their hand as an indication of interest you can consider whether they're capable of doing what you need. If they are that's great, but if not you can look at this as a professional development opportunity for the individual. Also, are you working with your leadership and development teams to ensure the person is identified as a good organizational citizen? Gaining recognition for enthusiasm and willingness to take on additional responsibility is a powerful motivator for many employees.

Suppose you have a requirement to improve the ethical sourcing in your supply chain. There's bound to be at least one person in your company's procurement department who's sick to death of filling out forms, and would love to be involved in sustainability planning or sourcing more environmental-friendly materials for the company. Giving them the opportunity to interact with their peers on a topic they know a lot, and participation, provides them with several benefits: they broaden their professional network, they get more task variety, and they have the opportunity to demonstrate leadership. In return, you gain an enthusiastic new team member who will need guidance but is also willing to learn.

Notes from the Field

Working Through a Merger: Yours, Mine, and Ours

Marlene M. Ibsen, Vice President, Community Relations,
The Travelers Companies, Inc.

Sometimes getting your team together can be more complicated than others. Travelers has grown not only organically but also through mergers and acquisitions. Experience has taught me that there are four practices to keep in mind when bringing two organizations together:

- Understand senior management's aspirations.

- Honor the previous work of both organizations.

- Listen closely to team members' ideas, leveraging their knowledge and experience.

- Employ "forthright diplomacy": straight talk that is both respectful and direct.

My most recent experience comes from my position in corporate philanthropy where, early on, we had to focus on merging two separate U.S. operations, and more recently are working with our colleagues in offices in Canada and the United Kingdom to establish common practices and priorities as a means of promoting the corporate culture internally and reinforcing brand identity externally.

It is important to understand the company leadership's priorities in terms of cultural values and norms. For instance, are there key themes or values that the merged entity is focused on and communicating to internal and external stakeholders (e.g., expertise, customer service, innovation, etc.)? The cultural vision for the organization will provide the foundation from which you will build your department's strategy in support of business priorities.

If you are in a corporate citizenship role, whether as the overall lead for ESG programs or sustainability or a subset of the whole portfolio, identifying the ideal state is a key step. What combination of programs, resources, advisors, and structure will support the company's business goals while aligning with the corporate culture? From there, you can begin to develop a framework — with targets and objectives — to achieve that ideal, establish processes, and cultivate an environment to enable the work.

To create a corporate citizenship strategy aligned with company values, you must evaluate existing programs from predecessor organizations against your new framework and take a hard look at whether they are effective tools for developing and sustaining the culture of the merged organization. Institute a discipline of challenging your own assumptions and those of others. Ensure you are encouraging open dialog from all team members, to take advantage of institutional knowledge and individual expertise that contributes to a strategy that will yield positive outcomes for your department and company.

Once you have determined direction, strategy, and programs, create a communications plan that takes the concerns and potential negative (and positive) impact on internal and external audiences into consideration. First step: approval from senior management; it is important to get input and buy-in from the top to ensure your plans are supported if the impending changes result in concerns being raised through other channels within the organization. For all audiences, be ready to explain the business rationale, which should include why the chosen initiatives are important to the company and its character.

Building from the key values of the organization gives you the starting place, and you can then evolve through a continual cycle of evaluating results and getting internal and external stakeholder feedback to ensure you are staying on the right track.

You'll have realized by now there's a channel which employees always tune into in these situations: it's called WIIFM (what's in it for me). If you can work out what your opportunity offers them, not only will you engage them more readily but you'll also broaden the network of people you can ask to work with you in the future.

THE RIGHT STRUCTURE

We're moving onto the third point in your system now. How do you create the right structure for your program?

If you're a department of three, for instance, you can't realistically expect only one person to be responsible for the execution of a huge project for a major company. Therefore, thinking closely about the networks of people you recruit, and how you deploy them in a structured way, is vital.

Let's look at an example. We've already mentioned how when Dave Stangis arrived at Campbell in 2008 he was charged with designing an overarching corporate citizenship strategy, complete with targets and goals in keeping with the values of this nearly 150-year-old company. The plan he developed was organized around four theaters of operation and leveraged a set of cultural norms that existed under previous CEO, Doug Conant, and a lexicon embedded within the culture at that time: environmental stewardship, interactions with customers and consumers, measurable community impact, and building an extraordinary workplace.

Each theater related to a theme built on "nourishing" (the company's mission at the time was Nourishing People's Lives, Everywhere Every Day): the planet, consumers, neighbors, and employees. They were also characterized by an audacious destination goal that was almost impossible to comprehend at the time, but which painted a clear picture of success. The goals were specifically designed to be clear and easy to understand, while also instilling creative tension and demanding change. In 2010, Campbell launched their original 2020 corporate citizenship agenda:

- *Nourishing Our Planet*: reduce the environmental footprint of our product portfolio by half, as measured by water use and CO_2 emissions per product.

- *Nourishing Our Neighbors*: measurably improve the health of young people in our hometown communities by reducing hunger and childhood obesity by 50 percent.

- *Nourishing Our Employees*: achieve 100 percent employee engagement in CSR and sustainability.

- *Nourishing Our Consumers*: continue to advance the nutrition and wellness profile of Campbell's product portfolio.

Campbell has continued to evolve with a new strategic framework anchored in its purpose — and its corporate citizenship strategy is evolving with it. No matter the point in time, you can see how important getting the necessary buy-in from a diverse range of business units and functions was in making the objective of good corporate citizenship just like any other business objective — one that would advance the company and deliver returns. Remember the purpose of a corporate citizenship strategy isn't simply to do good, but also to drive competitive advantage.

While it was determined from the start that top corporate officers must firmly guide the execution of the strategy, Dave still needed to garner support from wider constituencies across various units and brands. To do this he used the *Star Model* we talked about earlier. A pivotal step in the implementation of his strategy at the time was the establishment of governing committees across each theater; he created four executive steering committees that included professionals from across the business units to set and achieve goals. These committees created accountability and fostered the process component: conversation and collaboration enabling Campbell to achieve its corporate citizenship goals. Recognize that your corporate citizenship strategy and any related governance structure will evolve, much like Campbell's has over Dave's tenure. He is now leveraging an entirely new framework in partnership with CEO Denise Morrison and Campbell's purpose launched in 2014, Real Food that matters for life's moments.

You'll remember in the last chapter we talked about strategy being similar to generalship; it's the same with structure, in that you're marshaling resources to get tasks done. Effective structures provide the motivation for people to want to participate and support the processes for communication with them.

Many companies have created formal as well as informal governance structures around their corporate citizenship programs. Employee councils help provide feedback about the priorities you've set and, by consulting groups of employees in their arenas of influence, will provide feedback about what's working and what's not.

By the way, some of the best people to have in your governance structure are natural "boundary spanners" — employees who are well known across the company (often they've been around a long time) and have good relationships in different areas. If you connect with them regularly and ask them to contribute their ideas they'll feel a sense of responsibility and ownership, as well as giving you excellent feedback on your plans and campaigns. Not only that, when they're able to report successes back to your group, it helps reinforce your processes through comparison (a little healthy competition is never a bad thing).

Notes from the Field

Consider Corporate Citizenship Governance from the Beginning

Dave Stangis, Vice President of Corporate Responsibility and Chief Sustainability Officer, Campbell Soup Company

In my experience at Intel Corporation, later at Campbell Soup Company, and in multiple conversations I have had with my peers and other companies seeking to establish strategic corporate citizenship programs one key to success comes up time and again — that is to consider and establish a governance structure or structures that drive accountability and enable decision-making. Most companies, of course have organizations in place to manage human resources, finance, marketing, legal, operations, sales, etc., however the corporate citizenship agenda often cuts across many internal organizations and functions and almost always relies on decision-making and accountability outside of traditional organizational structures.

At Intel, I relied upon a management review committee (MRC) convention used at the company for many years. I established a Corporate Responsibility MRC that included key decision-makers and content experts from disciplines such as environmental health and safety, HR, legal, corporate governance, communications, government, and public affairs. This group was formally chartered with roles, responsibilities, and oversight functions. It met regularly and intersected with many other formal and matrix organizations across the company. It was critical in driving strategy, enlistment, and results — but perhaps most importantly, being able to weigh company opportunities and make decisions. This was also my sounding board and advisor group. At the time I put it in place, every member was my senior.

At Campbell, I built on those learnings and the Campbell culture to propose to formal governance structures: one at the most senior level of the company in the form of an ultimate steering committee, and one to oversee and drive the sustainability strategy. These team charters were drafted and shared with the General Counsel and CEO as part of my strategic plan proposal. These concepts were new to these Campbell leaders and they saw great value in the design. They asked me to create three more formally chartered teams that would help guide the workplace, marketplace, and community pillars of the corporate citizenship strategy for Campbell. Each of these teams also had formal governance charters, and were supported and staffed under CEO direction. While I directed the teams, the company's top executives in charge of the various functions were assigned as partners with me. These formally chartered teams, combined with CEO buy-in and support were critical to jumpstart early action and momentum.

Over time, the governance structures evolved in both companies as corporate citizenship strategies and programs matured. No matter where you are on your corporate citizenship agenda — creating from scratch or taking over a mature program, you have to consider and build into your strategy a governance system to drive accountability and decision-making to fully integrate corporate citizenship into the business operations.

THE RIGHT PROCESSES

This is the fourth element of your organizational ecosystem. How do you get your work done? Processes cover every element of your corporate citizenship program implementation, including the steps you're taking to recruit people to your team, how they're going to carry out the tasks, how decisions will be made, how you're going to communicate progress, and what methods you'll use to document those processes so others can replicate them.

You may be wondering what we mean by processes. Think of them as being like the directions section of a recipe. The same ingredients can yield very different results, based on the processes used to cook them. Take the processes you use to cook an egg: the procedure for boiling an egg is very different to that for frying an egg. You need to decide the outcome you want at the beginning so you know the best process to achieve it.

Here's an example. Suppose you work for a large retail chain that employs many workers who don't have regular access to computers. If you want to recruit a large number of them to participate in your corporate citizenship program, your process would involve going into the stores to talk with managers and associates face to face, or communicating with them via their newsletters or message boards. Whereas in a high-tech company you would be expected to communicate through digital channels. You use different processes to engage the same number of employees, but it will look different, depending on the environment.

Communication processes are obviously critical, but there are also execution processes. Take, for example, the green teams we discussed earlier. If you have ambassadors from all over your company who have offered to be part of your initiative, not all of them will be capable of executing your plan without support. Let's face it, many have probably never done anything like this before. So you'll need to provide them with step-by-step directions for what you want them to do, and support them while they execute it. Your process might include a timeline and sequence of tasks. Say you're instructing them to send an email to a certain group of people; it would be a good idea to include an email template for them to use. It could even be as detailed as telling them how to get onto the company's internal email system if they're not already (or providing the name of the person who can help them do that).

One of the processes Campbell has implemented to deepen employee involvement in their corporate citizenship program is to create an orientation module for all new employees as part of their regular onboarding. It begins by explaining what sustainability and corporate citizenship mean at Campbell, then goes on to provide information about how employees can become involved in the program and learn more. It's seen as a simple, low cost way to make everyone aware of the corporate citizenship mission and opportunities. Without this orientation, many people would spend months or even years wondering how to connect with them, whereas now they know what to do from day one. Dave has a small team at Campbell, but they can tell you, one of his mantras is converting people's passion to business process. It is the way to make corporate citizenship "stick."

You'll also need to decide where the lines of responsibility are drawn between your committees and yourself. Are you going to have meetings, and if so how often? Who is going to do what? Are they providing input, or are they decision-makers? Remember to document it so you know what works next time.

Which leads us to this: effective companies all have something in common when it comes to processes and procedures. Each time they create a new one they do an action review, asking "What did we do? What went well? What didn't go well? And how can we improve?" They then record this information so they can avoid reinventing the wheel each time. This essential but often overlooked step in creating your processes will save you and your team hours of wasted time and effort.

THE RIGHT METRICS AND INCENTIVES

The people you've organized to implement your processes are more likely to stay engaged with your initiative if it's clear to them how you will measure and reward success. Establishing agreed upon metrics is vital in that they communicate progress, so everyone can understand what's been achieved. There's nothing more demotivating than working hard on a project only to be left in the dark about what the end results have been, or even how it's progressing as time goes by.

Incentives for performance are, of course, a little tricky when you're managing people through influence (rather than by direct control) as you can't necessarily give them financial rewards. There are other incentives you can offer, however. One is a job well done; intrinsic motivations like satisfaction can be a powerful incentive to continue, and people like to carry on doing things they experience success with. Public recognition for achieving milestones can also be a powerful motivator, especially when it's conferred by your CEO or other key players in your c-suite.

Different employee groups are motivated by different things. If an early career employee who's very interested in developing their professional network is publicly praised for their contribution to a corporate citizenship project, and as a result, it comes to the attention of a top level executive, they can perceive that as more of a benefit than being recognized by their direct manager. For a more experienced employee, the reward would be more likely to come from getting involved in something bigger than themselves, which allows them to leave the world (and the company) a better place. It's part of their legacy.

This is good news for you, because you're unlikely to have a budget to reward people financially, but you can reward them in other ways. As part of its reward structure, Campbell has put in place an array of employee recognition programs for work related to sustainability and social responsibility. These have included peer recognition programs, and handwritten notes from the CEO, along with praise at employee forums and in articles on the company's intranet. There are also social responsibility components included in Campbell's *Greatness Awards*, which are their highest recognition for work done by individuals and teams. The CEO and corporate leadership present these awards annually.

As you get more sophisticated and your program matures, you can think about pay incentives. Among managers and executives, compensation is a growing part of the reward structure.[1]

Metrics and Measurement

It's worth taking a moment here to focus on how you're going to measure the results of your program.

The first questions to ask yourself are: what would you *like* to measure, and what can you *actually* measure? Depending on your capabilities and resources, you may not be able to measure all outcomes or even impacts.

Start internally. What are the key performance metrics of your strategy based on the work you've done so far in this book? Will you be seeking to assess your company's energy use, greenhouse gas emissions, waste generation and recycling, and water use? How about employee volunteer hours, training and development, and investments? Would you include product and service-related items, such as packaging improvements, sales from improved product lines, and consumer or stakeholder perceptions? Getting to the KPIs and baseline data for your company can be a major undertaking, so don't underestimate the time you'll need. You can, however, use some of these external resources to help you:

- The GRI Standards and sector supplements can be found at globalreporting.org

- Carbon Disclosure Project (CDP) can be found at cdp.net

- Dow Jones Sustainability Index (DJSI) assessment can be found at sustainability-indices.com

These three organizations provide standards and measurements for how companies are being measured against each other in their performance of the ESG dimensions of business. Each offers an indexed set of measurements that will help your company understand the state of current best practices in measuring ESG performance.

As discussed in the preceding chapter, no matter where on the trajectory of work you're able to measure, you'll create a better program if you decide the metrics and measures during the design phase.

THE ONLY CONSTANT IS CHANGE

And finally, remember one of the constants in business is change. A common reason why corporations seek our help at the Boston College Center for Corporate Citizenship is because there's been a change of top management and priorities are shifting. An alteration in strategy means you may need to adjust your whole organizational ecosystem for success (your star design) in order to address changes in personnel, strategy, or work processes. This can feel really daunting for a corporate citizenship director, and it can also be very unsettling for the team you've pulled together to help you execute your strategy. It may be a time when you pull back and focus on those elements of your program that are less aspirational and more focused on enhancing persistent operational goals, like keeping employees engaged or finding operational efficiencies. However, bear in mind every shift in organization or strategy can be a moment of opportunity.

Here's an example of a company which has been through major change in its corporate citizenship program in recent years: Walmart. In the decade 2000–2010 this business was extraordinarily influential in developing sustainable packaging and plant management, bringing in products like the compact fluorescent (curly) light bulb. This created not only environmental but also business benefits, because less packaging meant they could get more products on their shelves, increasing their sales per square foot and reducing shipping costs with products which were lighter and less bulky to transport. However, just when they were getting some great recognition for this, the media began to shift their attention to income inequality. So Walmart went (in the media's eyes) from being at the vanguard of the environmental movement to being seen as needing to address social issues in terms of their employment practices.

At that point they had to move their attention away from the environmental work (much of which was well embedded by then in any case) to the social side. Now they're developing programs to bring their high-potential employees into online learning, and innovating with a whole raft of social initiatives such as promoting low-cost fresh produce to lower income people. Their focus had to change, which meant the structure of their program had to go with it, and the people who are now the ambassadors for their social initiatives aren't necessarily the same people who were working on their environmental projects. As you can imagine, different capabilities were needed.

Alongside that, their metrics of success changed. Instead of being measured in kilowatts or tons of packaging saved, they're now measured in more human terms. This means their processes have changed as well, because they're now focused on the people who work for them, in addition to their products.

PULLING IT ALL TOGETHER

You can see the way to organize your plan is to track each of the five points of the star, because if even one of them is out of kilter you're not going to be able to get the work done.

If you've got good people and a great structure, but you haven't implemented a reward system, then you're not going to keep those employees on board with your program. On the other hand, if you have the right people and structured rewards, but no process for communicating them, then your projects won't be running effectively either. Each of the five elements is part of the network, and the good news is there's much more stability in this five-point system and in the network you develop.

WHAT WE'VE COVERED

- Building networks and personal influence is critical to setting up and organizing your corporate citizenship program.

- There are five key elements to address as you organize to execute your plan for success: the right strategy, people, structure, processes, and metrics and incentives.

- Thinking about "what's in it for me" is one of the best ways to recruit and motivate the best people.

- When change happens, work through the design for execution to determine what else you might also need to change.

10 QUESTIONS TO ANSWER BEFORE YOU MOVE ON

1. Have you drawn a map of your existing network — the people who can help you implement your plans?

2. Have you identified the people in your existing network who will serve as workers, ambassadors, and sponsors? Do you have a healthy number of each, and in the right places? What can you do to get a critical mass in key departments?

3. Have you worked out an influencing strategy for approaching and motivating the people in these new areas?

4. Can you describe your corporate citizenship structure? Have you created an organization that allows for feedback and

decision-making from key contributors? Do people understand their roles and the accountability they have to the project and each other?

5. Can you describe the WIIFM for each member of your corporate citizenship network?

6. Do people understand their roles and the accountability they have to the strategy/project and to each other?

7. What processes do you currently use, and how could they be improved? Are they documented? Does everyone understand how they should be implemented?

8. What metrics can you measure today? What metrics do you believe you need to measure that you can't measure today?

9. How will you communicate these metrics and measurements to your team?

10. Have you defined a set of incentives that you want to use or create? Which are in place now and which are part of your future plans?

NOTE

1. The Boston College Center for Corporate Citizenship (2015).

SECTION 2

GETTING RESULTS ACROSS YOUR BUSINESS

6

THE IMPORTANCE OF YOUR SUPPLY CHAIN AND PROCUREMENT FUNCTION

Your company's procurement and supply chain processes are the richest and fastest growing area for most companies to identify risks and opportunities for corporate citizenship programs. Your supply chain can hold the big challenges for a company's corporate citizenship performance and reputation, yet can also provide the most significant opportunities to address them. In fact, when students around the world ask us the best route to a successful corporate citizenship career, we often suggest they start in the supply chain area. There really is no better way to get under a company's operational and sustainability hood than to become an expert in how it sources goods and services. It's also the part of the sustainability and corporate citizenship world that's growing the fastest relative to the need for staffing and training; as a result, it's an area where there likely will be significant career opportunities.

You've probably heard the procurement function referred to as supply chain, procurement, materials, purchasing — all these terms describe the corporate functions that buy, trade, and procure raw materials and services for your business. Some of these purchases will be items your offices need to function, for example, electricity and IT systems. Others will be materials that go into manufacturing the products you sell. There may be various parts of your company that buy their own services independently as well, for example, marketing services, cleaning and sanitary services, and electricity.

Why is corporate citizenship so integral to procurement? Because for every material or service your company buys, there are issues to monitor and manage, from a risk and opportunity perspective. If you don't invest time in understanding your supply chain, there's an activist or advocate group that will be monitoring it for you. From human rights to climate change, from biodiversity to animal welfare, and from toxic substances to diversity in employment, there's a huge range of issues to contend with. Ethical supply chain management has also gone from being a reactive business discipline to very much a proactive one — it has to be. Ten years ago, if something went wrong in your supply chain your company would have days or even weeks to investigate and fix it. Today with the explosion of social media, you'll be lucky to have an hour. And you will probably not even be the first to know about it.

So get it right and you'll be a hero. Get it wrong and the consequences can be enormous.

It's complex.

Working with procurement is rewarding, but it can be incredibly hard to wrap your head around how complicated the issues are, and how broad the scope. Think about the big corporations you know — the brands that are household names. They have thousands of suppliers; even small companies will have scores of them. Unfortunately, you can't manage all these suppliers individually, but this chapter will help you find ways to prioritize and manage them.

To stay on top of potential risks, the main people to connect with are members of your procurement team who buy raw materials for the products you make. If you work in a food company, for example, some ingredients might be traceable down to the farmer who grows them. However, there may also be other ingredients, such as oils, grains, or starches, that are a mix of products from many different places, so transparency to the source can be extremely difficult. Companies may buy from one supplier who buys from another supplier; by the time consumers receive the end product there are multiple points in the supply chain where things can go wrong. It's up to you as a corporate citizenship manager to mitigate these risks. Manage the issues well, and you'll create competitive advantage for your company.

By the way, this will never be perfect; your supply chain is too complex for that, and issues change over time. Categorizing your risks is simply a way of helping you prioritize where to focus first, narrowing down that overwhelming complexity.

Sidebar 3: Influencing Sustainability Policy

INFLUENCING SUSTAINABILITY POLICY

Beyond internal reductions and conservation, companies also are stepping into the policy arena — not only supporting climate legislation and government action, but demanding it. In July, 2015, Alcoa, Apple, Bank of America, Berkshire Hathaway Energy, Cargill, Coca-Cola, General Motors, Goldman Sachs, Google, Microsoft, PepsiCo, UPS, and Walmart committed publicly to the American Business Act on Climate Pledge:

This initiative, as part of the U.S. administration's Climate Action Plan, will cut nearly 6 billion tons of carbon pollution through 2030 — an amount equivalent to taking all the cars in the United States off the road for more than 4 years. Chinese President Xi Jinping committed for the first time that China would peak their emissions by around 2030.

By signing the American Business Act on Climate pledge, these companies:

• Voiced support for a strong outcome in the Paris climate negotiations.

• Demonstrated ongoing commitment to climate action by announcing significant new pledges to reduce their emissions, increase low-carbon investments, deploy more clean energy, and take other actions to tackle climate change. Including ambitious, company-specific goals to cut emissions as much as 50 percent, reduce water intensity as much as

15 percent, purchase 100 percent renewable energy, and pursue zero net deforestation in supply chains.

- Set the pace for their peers.

Source: https://www.whitehouse.gov/the-press-office/2015/07/27/fact-sheet-white-house-launches-american-business-act-climate-pledge

HOW TO MAP OUT YOUR SUPPLY CHAIN

The first step is to figure out what you do and don't know, and also what your procurement department does or doesn't know. How much do you really want to discover about your supply chain? How far back are you interested in digging, and how well equipped is your company to do this?

This can be a daunting project but there is always something to learn. So where do you start? Think about your business and perhaps the one or two primary inputs to your final product or service. To start, pick one thing. It could be a product, it could be a service, just choose one element to trace back; this will give you an excellent sense of what you're dealing with. This can be a complex process. Consider a company like Walmart; they sell just about everything to just about everybody. The plastic in their toys, for instance, is manufactured all over the world, as are thousands of electronic components consisting of minerals that are mined in challenged economies with potential human rights abuses. The food they sell has potential risk exposure as well, from the use of palm oil and the resulting deforestation, to the possible existence of child labor in cocoa and coffee supply chains. Now you're starting to realize the magnitude of potential risks.

Once you've done this you're ready to map out your company's broader supply chain. You may find this has already been done, and if so you have a great starting point. If it has not, you should try to create a risk map of your suppliers, even if it's rudimentary. Think about how other companies within your sector would see their risks; for instance, if you're an electronics manufacturer your map might center on mineral extraction, child labor, and working practices in factories.

The next step is identifying groups of suppliers (or your inputs) by risk level. Group them into low-, medium-, and high-risk companies or materials. This will be of great help when you set priorities for the next few steps.

You can think about the risk inherent in your supply chain in a few different ways:

- Size of risk.

- Reputation impacts of the topic or area of risk to your customers or the community.

- Long-standing practices known to be risky or less transparent.

- Suppliers your company spends the most money with — is a large proportion of your spend with a few suppliers?

- Choice of suppliers — do you trade with companies that are the sole source of supply for a particular product?

- Geographic region — there are various risks inherent in different regions of the world.

Relative to your corporate citizenship discipline, there will be a list of risks that are well known within your sector; if not, you can do a little research and assess products for any specific risk in your supply chain. For example, in the food industry we know palm oil, coffee, and cocoa are three raw materials that carry human rights and environmental risks. Similarly, in the Congo and neighboring countries, mining for "conflict" minerals is an issue as these minerals are contained in almost every piece of electronics in the world and many types of packaging. There are numerous groups focused on minimizing the dangers inherent in this area. We've all heard about "blood diamonds" and sweatshop labor; each sector and supply chain has a unique and challenging set of issues. As you proceed to where your materials are grown, sourced, and produced, you'll find that this is where controversies and explosive negative media stories are most likely to crop up.

Notes from the Field

Supplier Responsibility and Codes of Conduct

Tim Mohin is Vice President of Corporate Citizenship at AMD and author of Changing Business from the Inside Out: A Treehugger's Guide to Working in Corporations. *He has led corporate citizenship initiatives at AMD, Apple, and Intel*

The trend toward outsourcing coupled with high profile cases of poor conditions in the supply chains of global brands has led to an explosion of interest in the area of "supplier responsibility." Stated simply, supplier responsibility is about holding ?suppliers accountable?to the standards of conduct expected by the customer.

Establishing your company's code of conduct

Supplier contracts typically include language mandating compliance with all applicable laws and regulations, but the social and environmental laws applicable to global supply chains vary from country to country. If the supplier is in a country where labor and environmental laws are inadequate or poorly enforced, the purchasing company could be exposed to liability. This is where a code of conduct comes into play. In essence, a code of conduct establishes a consistent "floor," or the minimum expectations for your suppliers, regardless of the locally applicable laws or enforcement.

Incorporating your company's code of conduct into supplier contracts typically makes compliance binding, provides audit rights, and obliges suppliers to correct deficiencies. Your supplier management program can be made stronger with attention to three basic program elements:

1. *Compliance*: Conducting audits and correcting deficiencies can be a large investment. Compliance is necessary but programs that are overly focused on compliance can diminish the trust and cooperation that are essential for performance improvement. One of the first compliance issues is how to prioritize suppliers for scrutiny. Most programs rank suppliers by the magnitude of their business relationship and the probability (based on geographic or other factors) that the supplier may present risk.

2. *Business integration*: One of the most effective strategies for supplier responsibility is to integrate the program into standard business processes — especially supplier selection; supplier business reviews (SBRs); and supplier?termination.

   Supplier selection is the most opportune time to inject responsibility into the relationship as that is when a supplier is working to get your business. By including responsibility as one of the areas that are evaluated in the SBR, it becomes a fundamental part of the business relationship. This process also exposes senior managers from both companies to responsibility issues.

   Supplier termination rarely happens solely because of responsibility issues. Nonetheless, it is important that responsibility criteria are included in the termination process to make it clear that responsibility is a critical part of the business relationship. Termination is not always the answer. If possible, it's preferable for the supplier to address the problem. By working with suppliers to resolve serious issues, the buying company can use their economic influence to sustainably improve conditions.

3. *Capacity building*: The goal is to give suppliers essential capabilities and self-sustaining systems that allow them to manage risk and opportunity for their business and for yours. Capacity building ensures that both managers and workers in supply facilities have the knowledge, skills, and systems to manage human and natural resources safely and sustainably.

With globalization opening access to markets with undeveloped regulation, many believe that there is now a "race to the bottom." The field of supplier responsibility turns this concept on its head. Companies are increasingly using their buying power to drive improvements in responsibility throughout the global supply chain.

WORKING WITH CODES AND STANDARDS OF CONDUCT

There are many codes of conduct that set rules to define what's ethical and responsible, and what's not. This means someone else has done work assessing and prioritizing risks in any given area, which can only be of help to you. Understanding these helps create an ethical supply chain approach in your business.

If your corporation is similar to most, you'll need to work with preexisting codes of conduct that outline the standards of behavior expected of your company and its procurement team. There are probably at least 50 different examples of third-party codes of conduct you should be aware of, and we'll be giving you some examples in this section.

Codes of conduct are basically mandatory and non-mandatory rules set up for how you conduct business and manage your suppliers (including how your suppliers manage their suppliers). You can see they're integral to help you manage risks in this area, although they're also very complex.

So where do these codes of conduct come from? Some will relate to your own company's behavior and use, drawn up internally by your ethics or governance functions, or your human resources or procurement team. Others have been created externally by an overwhelmingly long list of interest groups ranging from public bodies such as the United Nations (UN) and the International Labor Organization (ILO), to world governments, and charities like Oxfam, Greenpeace, the Rainforest Action Network, or the World Wildlife Fund. Some of these codes have become law, and some merely set expectations about the way humans, animals, and the environment should be treated. Importantly, most of the countries have a set of laws and regulations that govern core expectations. In the United States for example the Department of Labor, the Occupational Safety and Health Administration (OSHA), and the Environmental Protection Agency (EPA). The OECD tracks and makes available a useful database on international regulation (http://www.oecd.org/gov/regulatory-policy/irc-toolkit.htm).

Your own company almost certainly has some codes of conduct already in place, so that's the best place to begin. They may govern how you treat your workers, dictate how you assess environmental and health and safety issues, and place prohibitions on certain chemicals or types of ingredients. In fact, most progressive companies will have two sets of codes of conduct: how you behave as a company (e.g., communications, the prohibition of bribery and corruption, undue influence) and how you expect your suppliers to behave.

You may be lucky enough to find there's one person who manages all these codes in your company, but it's more likely there are many codes located around the business and you'll have to hunt them down. Once you've done that you can start to catalog all the codes of conduct your company needs to abide by, either because you've written them yourself, or because third parties have set them for you, based on the sector you operate in.

This list can get pretty long. For instance, many suppliers around the world work toward similar expectations in relation to human rights. Given that the UN and the ILO have standards for protecting and establishing human rights standards, it doesn't matter what business you're in — recognizing and having systems around the protection of these rights is universal.

It gets more specific in the environmental arena. The expectations here can be wide-ranging, going beyond compliance with local laws or even international conventions. So, it stands to reason your company standards may well be more rigorous than what's expected legally, and focus on the issues most important within your supply chain such as water or greenhouse gas emissions, waste, and other related factors.

After that there is a huge number of benchmarks set externally for the kind of business you're in. For example, in the food sector Oxfam is well known for review of the supply chain focusing on transparency, women, and children in the workforce, how people are treated on farms, the difference between small and large farmers, how land is managed, biodiversity, fertilizer use, and more. Advocacy groups like this do the research in the field and try to hold companies accountable, moving the needle a bit every year so companies like yours are continually encouraged to improve.

There are a couple of interesting examples in the electronics sector as well. One that focuses on technology products is Electronic Product Environmental Assessment Tool (EPEAT), which is a standard for how green a company's electronic products are. It takes into account how the components are made, how energy efficient they are, and where they come from. So governments, including the U.S. Government, can use a standard like EPEAT to help decide whether they're going to require computer purchases from a manufacturer that adheres to these guidelines.

You can see how these global and well-respected bodies set up expectations of behavior around the world. When companies want to show they respect human rights, for instance, they will often say they act in accordance with the UN Global Compact or the ILO Conventions.

In addition to external organizations (such as non-profits and the UN) creating codes of conduct, companies within the same sector are increasingly banding together to create their own. One of the first was the Electronics Industry Code of Conduct (now known as the Electronic Industry Citizenship Coalition or EICC). This was created by global brands such as Intel, Microsoft, and Motorola coming together to work with activists and NGOs in order to create a uniform set of expectations for human rights and environmental performance across the supply chain. They realized that, big as they were, the problem was too large for each of them to track and manage on their own. Now there are similar frameworks in place across the consumer goods world, including The Consumer Goods Forum, which is made up of hundreds of food and consumer goods manufacturers such as Unilever, Nestle, Danone, Campbell, and Procter & Gamble along with retailers such as Walmart, Marks & Spencer, Kroger and Walgreens/Boots.[1] The forum sets expectations on human rights and forced labor, environmental performance, and deforestation. In the apparel sector, Social Accountability 8000 (SA 8000) is a management system which was set up decades ago by the garment industry to minimize risks in its supply chain.

In addition to those listed above, one of the networks you should tap into is your own industry trade association. It will monitor relevant issues and risks for you, and will quite likely have a set of standards as well, so it's a really good resource not only for you but also for your buyers. If your company is a member of one or more of these associations, why not consider joining one of its committees or work groups as a way to further your understanding, build relationships, and increase your visibility in the process?

One final note: most manufacturing companies don't sell direct to consumers, they sell to some type of retailer, so retailers — including their own codes of conduct — have an essential place in the supply system. You'll need to be aware of their assessments and surveys because they may stop doing business in certain parts of the world (or with particular companies) they believe are too controversial or issue-laden.

LEGAL OR NOT?

As mentioned before, some of these codes are legally binding and some are not. Here's a good example of one that is legally binding.

The state of California passed a series of management and disclosure laws related to human trafficking between 2009 and 2012. The intent of the legislation was to eliminate human trafficking and slavery in the supply chain of anyone who does business in that state. Most companies doing business in California could happily look around their own offices and be comfortable that their staff are free to come and go as they please, but is that true across their entire supply chain? What about a situation where the purchaser does not know the source of an agricultural product, which is then mixed with other elements? Would every food company, for instance, know all the way down to farm level where their ingredients come from, or whether there are human rights abuses going on in the country where ingredients are produced? Some companies have already been sued for not fully complying with California's disclosure law.

This might seem incredibly onerous, and it is. In a moment, though, we'll help you work out how to build a system to manage it so you're able to set standards within your company — aspirational standards you will always work to improve upon.

In the meanwhile, here's a list of resources you can go to for help.

Resources for Social Expectations of Your Supply Chain

ISO 26000

SA 8000

OECD Guidelines for Multinational Enterprise

Core ILO conventions

UN Global Compact

The Global Reporting Initiative

Certain National Stock Exchange Listing Requirements

UN Guiding Principles on Business and Human Rights

The Global Social Compliance Program

SEDEX

Aim Progress

Resources for Environmental Expectations of Supply Chains

The Electronics Industry Citizenship Coalition (EICC)

The Consumer Goods Forum (CGF)

The Carbon Disclosure Project (CDP)

Responsible Care

INTEGRATING YOUR CORPORATE CITIZENSHIP STRATEGY WITH YOUR PROCUREMENT TEAM'S WORK

As you realize by now, a central theme of this book is the importance of embedding your corporate citizenship work into your company's existing objectives. Now you know the risks and opportunities present in your supply chain, and you have an understanding of the relevant codes of conduct. Next, you'll need to work out a way to integrate this knowledge into your corporate citizenship strategy. The process is similar to what you did with your stakeholders; your projects need to have supply chain requirements imprinted upon them. This will help your company develop more resilient systems to manage the risks inherent in your supply chain, and allow you to take advantage of inherent opportunities, as well.

One of these systems should be monitoring resources, or a list of the key topics and issues you want to keep abreast of. Now that you know what your company's procurement "hot buttons" are, you can start to tune into them. Set up Google alerts for the relevant keywords; do a daily sweep of your monitoring sites; join a membership organization or two which will keep you in the know; talk to your peers at other companies for support and guidance.

These are all ways to keep up to date, but given you now know what codes of conduct your company needs to follow, how are you going to actually manage the process to ensure it adheres to them? You want to find the person you can tap on the shoulder and ask, "Are you responsible for the behavior and performance of our suppliers?" Of course, that person may not exist, so what processes will you use to ensure the codes are properly communicated inside your company and to your suppliers, and is this even your job as a corporate citizenship person? Maybe it's the responsibility of the procurement team? Or does one sub-team focus on, for instance, environmental issues while another drives improvement around social standards in sourcing?

You also need to decide whether you will ask your suppliers to sign your company's code of conduct and whether you should conduct regular inspections. If this is the case, would you do the visit, or would you send a third-party inspector? Bear in mind there's a window of risk for whatever you do. So for your high-risk suppliers, for instance, you might visit twice a year whereas for your middle-risk suppliers it would be every other year. Your low-risk suppliers could just sign an affirmation. These are just examples for how you can adjust oversight and management based on risk, tolerance, and resilience.

The most important part is not just how you manage codes of conduct but how you set expectations, how you communicate them, and how you decide on the process to manage risk. Who owns and is accountable for that?

You can now see how important it is to build a risk map for your supply chain, so you can then decide how you might manage it. Remember, there can be tremendous value in teaming up with other companies in your sector so you can reduce this risk together. Conflict minerals is a great example. Many technology companies have come together as members of the Electronics Industry Citizenship Coalition to address this issue in their supplier code of conduct in order to reduce dangers in this part of their supply chain. Oftentimes, you can't do it alone.

An interesting aspect of being a corporate citizenship practitioner is you get to work inside your company to do all these things: build internal teams, raise awareness of the risks, and create and maintain high expectations; it is an influential position. Suppliers that bid for your corporation's business will come to know your standards, especially when those same standards are integrated into contracts with you. Most companies are not very advanced in this area — yet; so you get to be a pioneer. Only the biggest and best have it figured out (and even they struggle to keep on top of all the issues). You're driving business value for your entire company by helping it deal with these questions.

MOVING FROM RISK TO REWARD

When you first start to examine your supply chain, everything's going to look like risk; and, people being what we are, we're more afraid of risk than we are motivated toward reward. So you're bound to feel like your work with procurement is daunting, and that can lead to being in permanent react mode. You should try to avoid this. Your main opportunity is to move from being reactive to proactive, to help your company anticipate and prepare, and to find areas in which your company can differentiate itself from its competitors in a positive way. What do you want to be known for — not having anything "bad" going on, or for actually driving the agenda for change? You can see this particularly well in companies that source a single core ingredient such as cocoa, paper, or coffee. Because they rely so heavily on one kind of material, many of them have stepped up to help farmers create a more sustainable process for growing that also works economically for their customers, for example using fair trade or responsibly sourced ingredients.

That's the way you move away from being reactive or defensive — "We're on TV for _____" (fill in the blank here with any negative event that worries you) to becoming positively proactive and talking about the improvements you've made. One method of doing this is to score your suppliers for their performance and even to build a recognition program for your highest performing suppliers, which can motivate all to aspire to be the best. We'll go into this in more detail later.

PEOPLE ARE AT THE HEART OF YOUR SUPPLY CHAIN

Once you start looking at your supply chain from both an internal and external perspective, how do you train the people who manage it? How do you help your own company get smarter with its systems, so underlying issues don't develop into crises? We'll provide some examples of ways you can build a strong assessment system by working through the people within your procurement organization.

Corporate citizenship within your supply chain isn't just about standards and monitoring, it's about making your company more effective. And you do this through communicating expectations to your suppliers via your procurement team. Most companies have people in charge of buying one thing (or a group of things); there are usually individual buyers for metals, papers, natural resources, food ingredients, energy, and others. So how do you get the procurement managers of these services and products to be aware of the issues, to keep up to date, and to be trained on all the different angles of ethical supply chain management? Furthermore, what's in it for them?

You can have much more impact within your company by educating all the people who actually touch your supply chain, than you could possibly make on your own. There are many ways to do this: carry out periodic awareness training, create a newsletter or some other communication system, talk to senior management about creating an induction program for all new procurement employees — the list is as long as your imagination. You want to cultivate a culture in your procurement division, which sets an expectation that buying isn't just about finding the lowest cost, it's about strengthening the supply chain through responsible sourcing. This is a business opportunity, not a tax on the system. That way, your buyers go from being people who only negotiate for the best price, to pioneers who find opportunities in all their source materials.

Where do you start? Begin internally by equipping your colleagues with knowledge and awareness of emerging issues. Then begin to think longer term and focus more externally. Create a map of the activists and advocates in the specific risk areas, talk to them, and even set up meetings between them and the buyers within your company — it's a great way to educate both sides and cuts across the politics, removing the isolation many procurement people feel from the controversies a community or public affairs team might be dealing with.

Earlier we touched on creating a recognition system for your suppliers. This creates a win-win situation and can also reflect well on the buyer involved. By doing this, you're building a way forward for your suppliers to share where they're doing ethical work, helping you learn more and more over time. Your suppliers will love to be recognized among their own customers for building a sustainable, responsible, and resilient supply chain because it's a fantastic selling tool for them. A tiered approach, in which you recognize the best and encourage the others to aspire to match them, encourages your suppliers to compete around human rights, ethical servicing, and responsible sourcing, thereby helping you to manage your strategy with much more ease. McDonalds is one of the best examples of companies doing a good job of this in a systematic way; they put a lot of resources into annual recognition of their best suppliers, and publish the results widely.

So what form could a reward system take? Here's where you can get creative. It could range from verbal or written recognition to events, published articles, joint press releases, and other ideas. To really give it some gravitas, see if your Chief Procurement Office or even your CEO or President can get involved.

Your main ask, in mapping out your supply chain risks and opportunities, is to think about the social, human, and environmental aspects of how you source your products and services. It's an incredibly rich and diverse area, and one in which you can happily keep getting more and more expert over time.

WHAT WE'VE COVERED

- Procurement and supply chain management is one of the richest, most rewarding, and potentially most career-enhancing disciplines to work with as a corporate citizenship professional.

- It's hugely complex, with myriad layers of suppliers to consider, right down to the original source. You'll never manage to cover it all but you can try your best by focusing on the priority areas.

- Start by mapping out your supply chain and categorizing your risks into groups — this will help you begin the task of discovering what's most important.

- There's a huge list of codes and standards of conduct you need to be aware of, which can both help and hinder your efforts.

- You don't have to go it alone — there are many organizations that can help.

- Once you've done your mapping, your next task is to integrate the ethical issues you've identified into your company's supply chain management.

- Try to see it as an area for opportunities as much as for risk.

- People are the key to success, so you must include rewards for top performers in your ethical procurement strategy.

10 QUESTIONS TO ANSWER BEFORE YOU MOVE ON

1. Have you mapped out your suppliers and vendors through a formal process, assigning risks and opportunities?

2. Have you identified the key risk areas for both your business and your sector?

3. Have you decided how far back in your supply chain system you will go, or will you deal with first tier suppliers only?

4. Do you have a written code of conduct or set of supplier expectations that's easily available to your suppliers (actual and potential)?

5. Does your supplier code of conduct include expectations in the social (human rights, labor, community) and environmental (legal compliance, resource management, energy efficiency) dimensions?

6. What process have you identified for evolving your supply chain issues within your business and sector?

7. Have you defined ownership and accountability for ethical supply chain performance?

8. Have you identified and implemented a communications process to ensure your suppliers (actual and potential) understand and uphold your expectations?

9. Have you communicated and implemented an action program to deal with problem suppliers?

10. Have you established any capacity building components in your supply chain strategy, such as ongoing training or joint strategy development with key suppliers?

NOTE

1. For a full list, visit http://www.theconsumergoodsforum.com/about-the-forum/our-members

7

CREATING A MORE SUSTAINABLE OPERATION

In the previous chapter we helped you understand how to set up better ways of sourcing materials from your supply chain. In this chapter it's time to turn your attention inward to your own company and how sustainably it runs its own operations. In chapters 6 and 7, you'll notice we're taking a business flow approach — from the supply chain to the internal business as we discuss corporate citizenship. This order isn't set in stone. It may make more sense to you to focus on your internal operations before you address your supply chain. There's no wisdom in the particular order you dig into these areas, just that you think about them both in a strategic way. There are multiple opportunities waiting for you here — you just need to do a bit of digging to find them. In this chapter you'll learn how to choose the most productive areas to focus on, so you can make your business a model for your suppliers and competitors to follow.

Why should you go to this effort? Because it's the right thing to do of course, but that's not actually the main reason. The big incentive for you to take a magnifying glass to your own company is that there's a direct alignment between making it more sustainable and making it more efficient, profitable, and innovative. You have a golden opportunity to bring value to the bottom line, build competitive advantage in your marketplace, and develop your own business acumen in the process. Colleagues who until now may have been a bit skeptical about your financial or strategic contributions to the business will soon see your work with new eyes once you start delivering these results.

Going through this process systematically will also provide a deeper understanding of your corporation's internal functions; you'll discover how to work with key operational areas to become more sustainable and find ways to measure, track, and build upon this progress. Once you start shining a light on the key areas, people will pay more attention to them — which means they'll also focus on you and your corporate citizenship work. In addition, you can report on your improvements externally, which will in turn create more momentum and rapidly move you toward a sustainable corporate citizenship ideal.

Your company may already have an internal environmental team, and if that's the case you may be asking yourself why you need to get involved. Here's the reason: your role is to give your company a faster, fitter, more meaningful, and efficient way of thinking about the future. Even the most sustainably run companies in the world are trying to improve in the areas covered in this chapter. You'll probably be able to find additional opportunities, more than your environmental team colleagues will have the capacity to address; think of yourself as an internal consultant who helps them do their jobs better, expand their ambition and appreciate what's possible, as they deliver even better results. Your company has most likely been running its internal operations in a "business as usual" mode for some time, and this is your chance to bring a fresh perspective.

SETTING YOUR BASELINE METRICS

Before you start trying to improve your company's environmental efficiency, you need to find out how it's performing right now. How much energy and water does your enterprise use today? How much waste does it generate? How are your corporation's internal functions performing in the environmental realm as we speak?

In a moment we'll explain *how* to find the information you need, but for now just focus on *what* you're going to measure. Your corporation will already be tracking data such as sales, earnings per share, and cost of goods sold, so the basic mechanisms exist. The metrics you're looking for, though, relate to its inner workings.

Let's start with the big three: energy, water, and waste. You can't create a sustainability strategy without getting good baseline data on these, at a minimum. How do you do this? You find out who pays the bills and tracks usage (this might be an energy or compliance team) and ask them for the information. It isn't usually too complicated to get at least some of your data this way, even if it's only a start.

Once you know what to look for and where to find it, and have set up a measurement system to track it, you'll start finding opportunities everywhere you go. Through this you'll be driving a more sustainable business strategy, which over time will build your business' resilience and sustainability. As you progress, this will get faster and faster like a big flywheel. Think of your data as being the fuel that feeds the forward motion; as you know what to measure and share the results of your strategy, others see the value in what you're doing, which attracts support, which in turn provides more leverage in the business. Just be sure to give credit where it's due — to the teams driving and investing in the work.

You'll probably find delving into energy, water, and waste to be a challenge, but it's also an amazing exercise to help you understand more about your company's major environmental footprint today. We'll take each of these three areas in turn, below.

ENERGY

Energy feeds everything in your business, and with climate change and renewable energy getting so much attention there's a lot of opportunity to make sustainable changes. The term "energy" can cover elements including electricity, natural gas, fuels, and even steam. What's more, your company's energy use isn't only related to what it needs to run its base operations, it also covers the energy used by your suppliers as well as that related to the transportation of products and employees.

So how do you find out how much energy your company uses in its operations? Some companies may have this information available already (although not necessarily all in one place), and if yours does that's great for you, but even then you need to understand the context and what the numbers mean.

There are resources for this. If you are operating in the United States, the Environmental Protection Agency has tools to help you translate the information you find internally into greenhouse gas equivalents.[1] You can also check out the greenhouse gas protocol developed by the World Resources Institute,[2] and the information on energy published by the World Business Council for Sustainable Development.[3]

Your task at this stage is simply to figure out what you do and don't know. Try not to get bogged down in the complexity of it all — you'll never discover everything to do with your company's energy use. Just establish some principles and baseline measures which you will use. Ask yourself how well you can answer this question: how much energy does my company use, and where does it use it?

Sidebar 4: Microsoft Goes Carbon Neutral

MAKING CARBON NEUTRAL COST-EFFECTIVE

In 2012, Microsoft established an internal "carbon fee." It began charging its own business divisions for their carbon emissions based on their energy consumption including electricity use and business air travel. This dramatic move helped the company achieve its goal of carbon neutrality and net-zero emissions for its data centers, software development labs, offices, and other functions. "We instituted a carbon fee last year because it had the potential to ignite a culture change, and that's exactly what's starting to happen," says Rob Bernard, Microsoft's chief environmental strategist. "A carbon price means that we now have a common language for how to drive awareness around and begin to reduce emissions. It's made environmental sustainability an increasingly important part of how Microsoft does business." The carbon fee has helped support both energy savings projects at Microsoft and increased purchases of renewable power to make Microsoft the second largest purchaser of green power in the United States, according to the U.S. Environmental Protection Agency. The carbon fee also helped fund a new power purchase agreement Microsoft made to buy the energy from a new 100 MW wind farm in Texas.

WATER

Water is usually a simpler area to measure than energy. If your business isn't large, it might be as easy as pulling out your last few water bills. However, most big corporations derive their water from more than just one municipal source; they might get it from surface water (rivers, lakes, or streams), wells, recycled water systems, and gray water sources. Almost every major manufacturer on the planet has a significant need for water in every aspect of their production process.

Not only do you need to understand how *much* water you use, but also where it comes from, *how* it's used and where it goes once you've finished with it — how much goes into making your products, and how much gets recycled or pumped back into the original or alternate sources, or into municipal treatment systems.

WASTE

Waste is usually the easiest area to get baseline data on. Your business will almost certainly have a contract with a waste vendor or recycling facility, so it shouldn't be too difficult to measure how much waste is leaving the building, how much is being recycled, how much is going into landfill, and how much is going to a hazardous waste treatment facility.

Depending on what kind of business you work in, you might find there are more waste measures that are specific to your company or sector. For example, some manufacturers emit waste into the air. These substances go by various different acronyms which you'll have to learn, for instance VOC (volatile organic compounds), and NO_x and SO_x (oxides of nitrogen and sulfur). Particulates and ozone are key air pollutants and are the main precursors of smog around the world (e.g., think of the air pollution problems in Beijing). Understanding these details can get a little challenging when you're not a manufacturing expert, but just try to get your head around the top line information.

The great thing is that working out what kinds of waste your company is generating, and how it deals with it, are key measures that go straight to the financial bottom line. No business is in place to manufacture waste, so when you identify ways to reduce it that's a double win for your company and your community.

BRINGING YOUR METRICS TOGETHER

No matter what type of company you work in, you could potentially measure tens if not hundreds of inputs and outputs to do with energy, water, and waste. This would be a full-time job, and is of course totally impractical.

Instead, figure out the two to five major areas that are most relevant for your business. For example, if you're a timber company producing wood, paper, pulp, and corrugate, you might create a separate set of data for each output. One of your key business indicators would be the number of products you can make from a certain number of trees, and your objective would be to increase the volume of output for the resources you use.

HOW TO TURN YOUR BASELINE DATA INTO GOALS AND TARGETS

So now that you have baseline measures in place it's time to take action. How will you create goals and performance targets, based on the starting points you've identified?

First, do some easy benchmarking. Look to your peers and competitors if you need a quick level set on the key metrics for your own business. As a minimum you want to be able to assess and communicate the same types of environmental data your competitors use (and ideally you want to do better). All businesses love to compete, so you'll find your management team more than happy to engage when you share what your competition is doing on key performance indicators. Even businesses outside your sector can be motivational because they demonstrate what's possible.

CONTEXT-BASED GOALS

Before you go any further into goal setting it's helpful to understand new ways of thinking called "context-based," or sometimes "science-based," goals. Leading companies are evolving their reasoning around environmental goal setting, so instead of stating they're going to reduce their water use by 3 percent next year, they look at whether or not that makes sense in their business and geography. A corporation with a manufacturing facility based in the Arizona desert might create a more aggressive water reduction strategy than one operating out of Seattle or London, for instance.

This makes a lot of sense, both from a business and risk perspective. You may have read about the global environmental standards produced by agreements such as the Kyoto Protocol, or COP21. These aren't focused on a single company reducing energy use by 2 percent, rather they demand a reduction of greenhouse gases globally. More and more companies are looking at their goals and attaching them to this global context, rather than simply looking inward to their own performance.

This is much harder to envision than a simple, internal corporate goal. Everybody understands what a 1 or 2 percent reduction means, but signing up for some impact in society that's different in one place compared to another can be much more challenging. It might lead you to avoid sourcing ingredients from areas that are water scarce, for example. So although it makes sense to think about goals in this way because you're looking at the bigger picture, it's a lot harder to communicate in a language that's understandable to most executives. After all, they didn't go into business to worry about how their company will keep the climate from increasing in temperature by more than two degrees centigrade, did they? How would you measure the effect your efforts are having on the world? And how much could you claim "credit" for, if you're a food company compared to an automotive manufacturer?

This is still an emerging area, but over the next few years it's going to become a huge part of your job so it's a good idea to become familiar with it now.

EMPLOYEE HEALTH AND WELL-BEING

Increasingly, potential employees make decisions about where they want to work based on how safe they think their workplace will be, the benefits they will receive, and how good they perceive the culture to be in terms of taking care of their physical and emotional health. So you can see employee health and well-being is a key opportunity area for companies in the 21st century. Often it's overlooked, or allocated to departments such as operations or human resources, but even there it rarely gets the attention it deserves.

If you feel your company could do more to make itself attractive to employees (and which company couldn't?) this isn't something that happens on its own: you need to help drive the agenda. You're bound to have heard about the cool workplaces being developed in the tech world, which is creating a trickle-down set of expectations for all employees. Nowadays many businesses have fitness centers, in-house nutritionists, relaxing break areas, on-site childcare, parental leave, and other amenities, in order to create an environment in which employees enjoy working and feel safe.

How would you create baseline measures for these benefits or the amount of money your corporation invests in employee well-being, and how would you track it going forward? This is not an easy task, but depending on your industry there are obvious places you could start. If you're in the oil and gas sector, for instance, does your company have a zero tolerance for unsafe behaviors? If so, you'll need to set goals around them. That in turn means you'll need to ensure there's training around these expectations, and benchmarking to see how your business compares to others in the sector.

Of course you don't need to become an expert in health and safety, but you do need to help your company set targets and report progress. As you're no doubt aware by now, you have to know a little about a lot of things when you're a corporate citizenship professional. The more you assess the competitive landscape, the regulatory frameworks, and the cutting-edge technologies for all the topics in this book, the more you'll enjoy your job and the more value you'll bring to your company.

Finally, one of the most strategic things you can do in this area is to help communicate your health and well-being achievements to potential employees, your local community (which is where many of your employees will come from), and internally. Figure out which of these factors is a significant competitive advantage, so that your workplace becomes the place *everyone* wants to choose.

BUILDINGS AND FACILITIES

Believe it or not, your physical place of work is often the easiest and most effective place to start bringing corporate citizenship to life. If you think about it, putting a dedicated effort into improving the sustainability of your workplace not only pays cost-saving dividends, it can also play a key role in strengthening your company culture around your commitment to being environmentally friendly. Whether you work in a single building, a leased space, a network of buildings, or in a huge corporation, you can increase your sustainability in many different ways.

How do you go about this? Several resources exist to help make your workplace greener. These range from user-friendly technology to formal research. For information about building standards take a look at the U.S. Green Building Council's LEED standards; these focus on improving design and sustainability in the building itself. For technology there are smart systems you can investigate: sensors that turn lights on and off depending on whether people are around, temperature systems that know when people are in the building, and water-use devices that take gray water and recycle it, to name but a few. Even low-tech initiatives such as having different bins for recycling and regular waste are a step forward.

In terms of your actual offices, there are all kinds of opportunities for improving sustainability in furnishing and furniture, building materials, seating, desks, and technology. Each one of these has a sustainability story behind it. Remember, your company's employees are its best ambassadors, so if you want it to have an environmentally friendly image on the outside, you need to reflect that from the inside by walking the talk.

You have multiple chances to create an internal culture of sustainability using company signage and notices. How about highlighting your community activities and corporate citizenship achievements visually, in the entry lobby and hallways? Actually, it's often employees themselves who have the best ideas about how to make their workplace more environmentally friendly. You could crowd-source suggestions from them. This could be as simple as having a suggestion box, or as technical as creating an online platform which allows people to rate ideas. Experience shows an effective way to achieve improvement is to give employees accountability for implementing their own suggestions; if they have the assignment to figure out what they want in a cost-effective way, they'll own the idea as well as need to sell it, which means they'll feel motivated to make it come to life.

TRAVEL AND TRANSPORTATION

Unlike buildings, travel isn't something you can "see" which is why most people overlook it. However, it's actually a part of your workplace facilities and impact.

Take commuting for instance — there are many things you can do to promote greener options. This could range from company parking spaces dedicated to shared pool cars, or providing incentives for people to bike to work. Charging stations for electric cars have become expected, and many electric utilities will install these for zero or low cost. When you multiply the incremental environmental benefits for one employee by thousands, you can see how this can be an area of high impact.

You can also build recognition systems for community involvement around sustainability. Almost every local municipality in the developed world has some kind of local partnership in which they're working with companies to share best practices — yours is bound to have one. Consider other local businesses, or merchants where your employees may shop, as potential partners for your employee-focused programs. For instance, a local car retailer could offer your employees discounts on electric or hybrid cars, or the local utility may have discounts on roof-mounted solar panels. Don't forget to find a way to highlight employees who take advantage of these benefits.

Stepping back from individuals, let's look at business travel and fleet management. Most travel agents have efficiency programs you can implement. Each time they book a flight for an employee they can show the greenhouse gas impact of it in the itinerary; at that point either the employee or their company can choose to offset the impact by paying a small premium, or planting trees, or some other parallel offset activity. At the end of the year the agent can report how many miles your company has flown and even what the CO_2 emissions were. It's a great piece of information to communicate the fact you're monitoring it, and also to prove you're making positive changes.

Even rental car operators can help you identify greener options in your company fleet; there's a lot of innovation out there to help you, and it's usually free — just ask. Courier contracts are another place to look for improvements. The big firms have amazing schemes that can help you build sustainable practices that save costs and energy, such as grouping collections into certain days of the week. Even large office supply companies have environmental sustainability strategies to help corporations, and they're just waiting for your call. On the broader logistical front, there are many other tools. For instance, there's an external framework for the U.S. Environmental Protection Agency called SmartWay, which is a certification for road trucks covering a range of areas from fuel efficiency to aerodynamics; you can ask your suppliers to ensure their trucks are SmartWay certified.

So you can see how much free help is out there for you to access. The beauty of it is that it's incredibly measurable and cost efficient, a win-win for both you and your corporation.

SUSTAINABLE PACKAGING

If you work for a consumer goods company, or any business manufacturing a physical product, the packaging you use is a key opportunity for environmental advantage.

Like all the changes we've talked about in this chapter, packaging doesn't become sustainable on its own; you need an overt strategy, and it's not an easy area. Although there are cost benefits for companies in, for instance, making their packaging lighter in weight, the consumer is looking for convenience. We've grown to love individually packaged products especially when they're shipped from online retailers; everything comes in its own little box with its own bubble wrap. So unlike transportation or even energy, where moving to a more sustainable system is always win-win, packaging can be more challenging to improve. That's why you need to be very deliberate in how you tackle it.

The key to this is to partner up with your packaging suppliers and vendors. Agree to a set of goals and ask them to incorporate, for example, recycled materials wherever possible. Another option is to reduce secondary packaging (that's packaging which goes around the original to keep the product safe during shipping or distribution), or to send the packaging back to your supplier for recycling once you've received the goods. There are lots of ideas you can implement, and it can be a great opportunity to be imaginative. Just don't forget to keep track of the data and measure your progress. You don't want to eliminate a million pounds of packaging and miss the chance to communicate your environmental and bottom line savings.

One way to make this simpler but also generate tremendous value is to create objectives during packaging redesign or at critical packaging decision points. This means every time a product is being reviewed and its packaging redesigned, someone takes the time to determine if it can be made lighter in weight, more renewable, or recyclable. Just asking these questions can go a long way toward transforming your business's packaging footprint. They won't get asked on their own, though — you need baseline measures, a strategy, and longer term goals in place before product managers implement it.

There are plenty of resources to learn about different types of packaging materials. Most of the fiber, plastics, glass, and metal trading associations have life-cycle assessments for their packaging, along with advice on how to move to more sustainable options. In the United States, the Sustainable Packaging Coalition is one of several groups that highlights and promotes environmentally friendly packaging opportunities, as do trade groups for every type of material.

Although consumers value convenience, they also love the message recycled packaging sends to them; it's a clear indicator the company is serious about sustainability. As a result, it's one of the most straightforward ways to send a credible environmental message without spending money on advertising. You're demonstrating to consumers on an individual basis; you're not just *saying* the right things, you're actually *doing* them. One of the most notable examples of this happened when Dell began developing packing from 100 percent compostable mushrooms and straw. The package was so benign to the environment, it was literally edible and company founder Michael Dell demonstrated it as such when he ate a bit of it dipped in soy sauce in front of a sustainable business audience in 2015.

THE CYCLE OF INNOVATION

You are aware by now that tackling your company's internal environmental footprint is an innovative process, where you work alongside diverse external and internal functions to change processes that may have been in place for decades. Tapping into the innovation cycle is absolutely critical if you want your work to embed itself in the overall innovation process. If you don't do this, you'll forever try to keep up with people who have agendas that aren't necessarily aligned with yours.

Somewhere in your company is a person or group responsible for innovation and creating new ideas. These teams can be hard to find and may come under names that don't obviously link to innovation; they're usually related to corporate strategy, research and development, or possibly product development or marketing. If you're in a huge organization working across various sectors, innovation and strategic processes can be spread across different parts of your business. Developing a consistent, enterprise-wide approach to tapping into how innovation is done is probably not in your job description, but determining how to integrate your ideas into the process can provide additional benefits. While it's difficult to initially insert yourself into the innovation process, it will save time and energy later, and means you won't have to be there to "force" it, each time. It will simply happen, and the impact will multiply as the years go by.

For instance, why does your company use one transportation or packaging supplier instead of another which offers more environmentally friendly products or services? If you can find out when this kind of decision is made, who makes it, and how it's measured, you're able to influence a process that can deliver a larger and longer lasting impact.

Now you're starting to embed corporate citizenship into the innovative cycle of your corporation. In time, you can go from simply reducing energy and water use, to influencing what gets funded for a capital project and even the characteristics of companies considered for mergers and acquisitions. For instance, when a new building is being planned, employee well-being and sustainable design criteria can be considered as part of the process, rather than an afterthought.

If you put these leadership and management strategies in place within your corporate citizenship strategy, you'll start to create real value and position your company for the next century, while building competitive advantage for your company. It's a long-term effort and one of the toughest areas of your job, but it's essential. It's an achievement that will remain in place long after you've been promoted to your next role.

WHAT WE'VE COVERED

- Make your internal operations more sustainable, which has environmental and cost-saving benefits for your company, and career benefits for you. It's a treasure trove of opportunities.

- Set baseline metrics so that you can then develop goals and measure progress.

- Create metrics in the big three areas of energy, water, and waste.

- Improve employee health and well-being to help with employee recruitment and retention.

- Other opportunity areas include buildings and facilities, travel and transportation, and packaging. Improving the sustainability of each will improve both your company's reputation as environmentally friendly, as well as profitability.

- Embed your initiatives into the cycle of innovation in your company; although difficult at first, it pays rich dividends in the long run.

10 QUESTIONS TO ANSWER BEFORE YOU MOVE ON

1. Have you defined the core resource footprints of your enterprise (energy, water and waste use, waste generation, and emissions)?

2. Have you determined baseline measurements for your enterprise for those key resource footprints?

3. If you're a major player in your sector, do you understand the concept of context-based or science-based goal setting?

4. Do you have clear expectations that your workplace should be safe and healthy, and supporting practices and measures that are clearly communicated?

5. Have you employed practices and technologies in your work-place to drive energy and resource reductions, as well as to build a culture around sustainability? For example, have you

evaluated your travel and transportation activities from both an employee and supply chain perspective?

6. Do your employees have a clear way to provide input to your workplace corporate citizenship strategies, and to celebrate their successes?

7. Have you evaluated your packaging footprint from both a purchasing and marketplace perspective? Do you know your baseline? Have you identified opportunities to drive a more sustainable packaging footprint?

8. Can you describe the key processes and where most important decisions in your company are made around workforce development, material procurement, business operations, product development, and delivery?

9. Have you incorporated simple, comprehensive corporate citizenship and sustainability considerations into these business decision processes?

10. Have you established accountability and governance for enterprise-wide decisions relative to sustainability?

NOTES

1. https://www.epa.gov/research/methods-models-tools-and-databases

2. http://www.ghgprotocol.org/standards/corporate-standard

3. http://www.wbcsd.org/publications-and-tools.aspx

8

DEFINING AND MANAGING YOUR CORPORATE GIVING PROGRAM

Many people assume corporate citizenship is primarily about a company's corporate giving program (that's before they've read this book, of course). Actually, your corporate giving is simply another opportunity for your company to create business advantage while creating good in the world. Like corporate citizenship, the semantics around this practice are complicated. There are many ways to describe corporate giving: shared value, impact-investing, strategic philanthropy — just to name a few. As we are writing this book there are probably five new terms being developed to describe the practice. Don't worry about what you call your program.

Corporate gifts managed in a strategic way add value to society and for your company and may also allow your company to improve your operating context by using the assets at its disposal. The most effective corporate giving programs invest in causes and issues that are important to the company's community, employees, customers, and others in your operating context. Developing corporate giving and employee involvement programs that address issues important to these key stakeholders and arenas is an effective way to create value for the business and the community.

There should be an obvious, logical connection between your corporate giving strategy and your business strategy — one that's obvious to all your stakeholders — and not only those who actively engage in your program.

Your stakeholders should be able to discern why you're investing in one particular purpose and not another. If you can do this, you've reached a strategic "sweet spot." What's more, if there's a strategic fit, you'll be able to describe your giving program in a clear and understandable way. What are you trying to accomplish? For whom, and through whom?

How do you decide what type of corporate giving program to implement? The best place to start is to determine who you most want to affect with your corporate citizenship and what outcomes you're trying to deliver. Think about who you need to activate to create the best impact for your business and your community. If it's employees you most want to engage, start by thinking about what matters to them. If it's customers you want to connect with, then pick a cause they would easily associate with your business purpose. This can lead to a diverse portfolio of interests. At first this might seem like a contradiction to what we've said above, but it's not, so let's explain.

WHEN IS SMALL BIG?

For most companies, there's a combined need to support causes that connect to business strategy, *and* to invest in charities that are dear to employees' hearts, or that address critical needs in the communities where they operate, but which are otherwise unrelated to the business. Each type of giving has a role to play. In fact, giving to causes that connect to employee interests but not to the business strategy can actually support the strategic goal of improving employee engagement, and at the same time encourage employees to connect their personal values to the corporate values. There's real business benefit in that. When we at the Boston College Center for Corporate Citizenship see companies making large numbers of small donations that frequently tells us they're driven by a desire to match their causes to what their employees care most about.

For instance, we work with many companies that support organizations relating to science, technology, engineering, and mathematics (STEM) education, because it's a way for them to invest in the future workforce. Many of these companies may also be donating to disease prevention and health and human services charities because these are organizations their employees are involved with. This means the company's giving program has a portfolio approach to corporate giving. This is an entirely valid approach. There are no "bad" gifts, after all. Most companies, even if they did nothing to change this approach, are accomplishing plenty of good in the world with a more distributed giving approach. They are simply missing the opportunity to create strategic value for the company while doing good for society.

Sometimes these more distributed approaches can do good in ways that are incidental to the original purpose of the gifts. An example of this is companies that build recognition programs to encourage employee engagement with giving campaigns. The company can create value from this distributed approach by celebrating employee participation and leadership. Employee recognition is a crucial ingredient to deriving business value from many small, unfocused gifts.

Other ways to encourage employee engagement are to increase investments in causes favored by employees, matching employee gifts when possible, and asking their opinions on potential programs. If you're totally focused on STEM education, for example, and your employees are privately giving to food pantries/banks and cancer support, you have ways to acknowledge their priorities without requiring a financial gift. Why not invite employees to contribute to the decision about what partner you choose, or increase the matching gift when their giving aligns with the company's cause? Recognition and participation incentives drive more impact by enhancing employee engagement and ultimately retention, strengthening local communities, and your license to operate; well-publicized programs can even enhance your reputation and position in the marketplace.

As with all other elements of your corporate citizenship, your corporate giving program should be designed to advance one or more elements of your business strategy and to influence specific stakeholders.

TRENDS IN EMPLOYEE GIVING

More than 75 percent of companies report offering employee giving programs as part of their overall corporate giving programs.[1] The most effective programs are designed to offer employee choice and year-round giving options as well as payroll deduction and reporting. In addition, we see the following trends emerging among those companies that report the best outcomes from their programs.

PROVIDE ENGAGEMENT OPPORTUNITIES FOR VARYING EMPLOYEE SEGMENTS

Employees at different stages and levels are motivated to give and participate in corporate philanthropy and volunteer programs differently. Recognizing this, companies are offering more choice in their programs. Employees on a leadership track, for example, may be motivated to participate in a company's philanthropic strategy for the recognition, the exposure to executives, and the leadership opportunities. More junior employees may be more inclined to give time and to participate in employee-directed activities.

Notes from the Field

Nonprofit Board Service: The Triple Win

Anne Gross is Director of Corporate Responsibility for KPMG U.S.

Many nonprofits need technical expertise and help to keep their organizations running smoothly — and businesses are in a great position to help lend a hand. As part of our firm's commitment to improve the communities in which we live and work, KPMG encourages our leaders to serve on nonprofit boards. Multiple benefits are realized, including:

- *Supports the community*: Nonprofit board service leverages the business skills and insights of our professionals for the benefit of society.

- *Enhances skills*: Board service provides a hands-on opportunity to handle board-related governance issues and develop leadership skills.

- *Builds the network*: The intersection of business and civic relationships through nonprofit board service provides opportunities to expand personal networks and enhance KPMG's visibility and brand recognition in the marketplace.

Given what nonprofit board service has to offer, we integrated into our corporate responsibility strategic priorities and set a goal of having a majority of our partners and managing directors serving. First, it was important to know who was currently serving — where are the KPMG people adding value and what should our goal for the future be? Also, we decided that board service information should be a part of CRM (client relationship management). To measure how networks were being expanded and enhanced, it was evident that we should track nonprofit board service alongside information about our primary stakeholders, individuals in the market that are known to KPMG professionals. Once the nonprofit board service role was baked into the CRM system, we had to populate the data and ensure that our people are recording time incurred in nonprofit board service.

Secondly, we supported our professionals to pursue their personal interests and passion through nonprofit board service readiness training.

KPMG has an award-winning training and development program, so we connected with learning and development colleagues to prepare the necessary materials and course work. We then leveraged the knowledge and insights of our people that had a history of nonprofit board service along with our Audit and Tax professionals who provide compliance services to nonprofit clients. Working with these resources, and using third-party insight from *BVU: Center for Nonprofit Excellence*, we developed a training program that can be offered at various levels of depth and in a variety of training contexts.

In the first six months of offering nonprofit board readiness training, more than 500 professionals participated and were motivated to get involved to serve on a nonprofit board. We do not place professionals or guarantee that any financial obligations of nonprofit board service will be met. We are helping our people recognize the value of service and how they can identify organizations and support causes for which they have passion and interest, and in doing so improve our communities.

LEVERAGE TECHNOLOGY TO DRIVE ENGAGEMENT

The introduction of more choice certainly brings opportunity for companies and their employees to express shared corporate and personal values through workplace giving campaigns. Some of the innovations in campaigns that have been enabled by better technology have presented challenges to the traditional community affiliates. The level of engagement with federated giving organizations varies significantly by geography. Federated campaigns (and organizations) are not being abandoned, but they are being challenged to change the way they solicit and operate.

Similar to volunteer programs, workplace giving can have a positive impact on employee attitudes toward their companies. According to a 2013 study, participation in giving programs can help employees identify with their organizations more as a whole, which in turn can improve commitment and loyalty.[2]

In addition, a 2008 study found that employees who participated in a giving program experienced increased job satisfaction as a result of stronger commitment and an improved perception of their companies.[3]

Remember, being supported by a large corporation's employees, even if only in a small way, can be enormously beneficial to a nonprofit organization. Corporate gifts can help nonprofits build a wider support base, especially if employees are able to get more involved with the organization through volunteering in addition to a company financial contribution. Employee volunteers will feel more personally engaged with your cause partner and might spread this awareness to their friends and family, bringing even more supporters on board. So although the individual donation by your company may be small, the impact could be much greater.

This is in addition to the credibility bestowed upon the receiving organization through the connection they have with a well-known corporate funder.

MOVING TO STRATEGIC GIVING

Though all of these approaches offer benefits, the greatest of these to your business, your cause partner, and your community comes from philanthropy that connects the purpose and commitments of your company with a relevant cause that delivers a measurable societal impact. This is called a lot of things in business journals such as "shared value," "collective impact," or "strategic philanthropy" to name just a few. Examples would be a beverage company supporting water organizations, confectioners helping develop human rights safeguards in the sugar or cocoa supply chain, or IT companies investing in programmer diversity and STEM education programs. In each case the cause is related to an operating context issue which enables the company's success and requires a strategic partnership to unlock important benefits. These types of programs typically develop over years, and often from ideas that emerge from smaller partnerships.

The tricks to deriving the most benefit for all are:

- Make the connection between your cause and your company so obvious and logical that it would be evident to almost anyone who hears about it. When this is the case, stakeholders will assign more credibility to your company for commitment to the issue, as well as for having the expertise to make good investments.[4]

- Be upfront about the fact that your cause is important for society *and* your business. Research shows this also builds trust among your stakeholder groups, as they see your commitment as both strategic and as an authentic commitment.

- Invest for the long term. At the Boston College Center for Corporate Citizenship, we see the longer that companies invest in their signature causes, the more successful they are in achieving the business and social objectives of the giving commitment. Additionally, the longer you invest, the more likely your stakeholders are to remember your program, and the more they can see how committed you are to your cause. This can lead to many business benefits, including increased trust and also more sales.

DOES YOUR COMPANY NEED TO ESTABLISH A CHARITABLE FOUNDATION?

Once you've thought through your corporate giving program strategy, you'll need to work out which vehicles you'll use to make your philanthropic commitments.

Many companies ask us if they need to set up a charitable foundation to implement their strategy. The short answer is probably not, unless you work for a highly regulated industry such as pharmaceuticals or medical devices (which have strict rules governing how much influence they can exert in related areas), or want to make grants to individuals (a scholarship program or prize, for instance). You might also want to consider a charitable foundation if you intend to create a permanent endowment to support your corporate giving, or plan to solicit gifts from others in support of your cause priorities. However, unless you fit one of these criteria, you can probably do everything you want through a strategic corporate giving program, rather than establish a stand-alone, legally structured private foundation.

Companies usually give cash from one or more of the following three areas: a corporate budget line, through a corporate foundation, or through a supporting organization's donor advised fund (DAF), which is a designated fund within a nonprofit charity.

If you do give to a DAF your gift to the fund is to the DAF rather than directly to the causes you ultimately support. DAFs are intermediaries. Most DAFs will acknowledge the original donor when it directs the gift to a charity, but at the end of the year the "hard credit" for gifts accrues to the DAF. Some corporations choose to work with these intermediaries because they want to keep a distance between themselves and the recipient for various reasons, or because they have a need to realize the tax benefit from those gifts before they're ready to decide how to allocate them.

Here's an at-a-glance comparison between corporate and foundation giving; it's just for general information and does not constitute legal or tax advice. Use Table 6 to make a pros and cons list about your organizational options and always get an opinion from your company's general counsel.

Table 6: Corporate Giving Programs: Do You Need a Foundation?

Activity	Corporate Giving Program	Corporate Foundation
Hire staff	Staff may be hired	Staff may be hired
Make institutional pledges	Yes. A corporate giving program can make multiyear commitments	Yes. A foundation may make pledges for multiyear commitments, but may not fulfill personal pledges made by officers of the foundation or executives of the company
Create grant agreements	Yes. A corporation may make conditional grants, major gifts, grants that involve naming rights, complex assets, or multiyear programs	Yes. A foundation may make conditional grants, major gifts, grants that involve naming rights, complex assets, or multiyear programs
Convert to another type of charitable vehicle	Yes. A corporation can choose to establish a foundation at any time in addition to operating through its own budget	Foundations may dissolve and spend down their charitable assets through grant-making. Foundation assets may not be reverted to the company
Meet federal minimum distribution requirement	No. There are no minimum requirements in the United States for charitable giving among corporations. Such regulations do exist or are under development in other nations, including India and South Africa	Yes. In the United States, the IRS requires private foundations to meet an annual 5 percent minimum distribution requirement based on the previous year's net assets
Make gifts to individuals and families	Yes, though this may be a taxable expenditure. The recipient may also be subject to tax	As per corporate giving program, although a foundation may only make grants to individuals under certain conditions
Give to international organizations	Depends. Several countries have tax treaties with the United States that allow gifts to be made and charitable deductions to be taken as long as income is earned in those countries. In other cases, you may need to seek a foundation or supporting organization to help distribute funds internationally, to stay in compliance with the law	Yes. A foundation can make grants to overseas charities and nongovernmental organizations that serve a clear charitable purpose as long as they are compliant with federal laws and regulations governing international giving

Provide scholarships	Yes, though this will likely be considered a taxable expenditure. The recipient may also be subject to tax	Yes. A foundation may provide scholarships, fellowships, and awards as charitable contributions based on IRS guidelines
Engage in Program-Related Investments (PRIs)	Depending on the investment activity, the PRI may be considered a taxable expenditure	Yes. A foundation may engage in a variety of innovative ways to fund organizations, including loans, loan guarantees, and equity investments. PRIs earn returns for the foundation and are recycled back into the giving pool, so they do not drain assets like traditional grants
Appoint a board of directors or trustees	No. Although advisory committees may be formed, the fiduciaries of the company (and all of its activities) are the members of the board of directors	Yes. Once the foundation is established as a legal entity, the donor company must appoint a board of directors and establish operating rules and procedures
Manage the grant-making process	Yes. A corporation can establish its own procedures for soliciting, receiving, reviewing, approving, and following up on grant proposals	Yes. A corporate foundation can establish its own procedures for soliciting, receiving, reviewing, approving, and following up on grant proposals

Department of the Treasury, United States Internal Revenue Service Publication 526 Cat. No. 15050A.
Department of the Treasury, United States Internal Revenue Service Publication 4221-PF (Rev. 8-2014) Cat. No. 49830S.

DEVELOPING STRATEGIC PARTNERSHIPS WITH NONPROFITS

Now that you've decided how to structure your corporate giving program, you'll need to select and manage the partners you want to work with. You've been through your materiality/stakeholder assessment and engagement, you've analyzed your company's business strategy, you've prioritized issues, you've developed an overarching corporate citizenship strategy. You have narrowed the focus of what you are going to do and in what order. Say the issue you want to address is water. You'd like to develop a signature program related to water, and there are thousands of organizations that address water stewardship. The first step is to narrow the pool to those organizations that are working on the aspect of water (or arts or education) that is relevant to your program.

Nonprofits are differentiated in much the same way that companies are. Ask others working in the space who they respect, where the best thinking and implementation are happening. Spend time doing research. Go to conferences on the issues you seek to affect. Ask independent foundation colleagues who span the boundaries of corporate and NGO culture. This is where it gets hard, but it's also where the strategic impact happens. Once you have a short list, work through the following questions to determine what your strategic giving program will look like.

1. *What's the focus of your giving?*

   To answer this, it's worth asking yourself some further questions:

   o *What's* the issue you're seeking to address? Environmental concerns, education, arts and culture, or something else?

   o *Where* will your action be directed? At home or abroad? Globally, regionally, or within a country or community?

- *Who* will it help? A specific age group, gender, or population such as rural or ethnic?

- *Why* is addressing this issue important to your business?

- *How* will you address it? How much should you give? Should it be based on need, available funds, time, networks, or experience? Will you act alone or as part of a network with other funders?

2. *What should your company give, and how should you give it?*

Cash is the obvious gift, but how about expertise, knowledge (intellectual capital), or products? Employees and suppliers can also contribute by giving time or money, or even business-related resources such as supplies, space, or infrastructure support.

3. *Why is your company uniquely positioned to support the mission of this nonprofit partner?*

Your firm needs to have a logical connection to your partner in order for it to be viewed as credible by your stakeholders. This strategic connection can come from a market opportunity, your operating context, your employee interests, or from a disaster or other event that affects people or places important to your business. Ask yourself:

- Does this partner share your company's focus, and a vision for how the issues to be solved can most efficiently be addressed?

- Are they a good brand and culture fit?

- Are you and the nonprofit aligned on the ultimate outcomes you seek to deliver?

4. *What's their capacity to deliver?*

Does this partner have a track record of delivering results on similar projects, and do they have the financial resources, staffing, and technical capacity to achieve the goal you've set? What do other funders say about working with them?

5. *What's their financial health?*

    The first step is to check out your potential partner's website. The best charities are transparent and accountable to the public, so you should be able to see evidence of this on their website. Can you easily find information about their staff and board of directors? Have they published financial information such as their most recently filed Form 990 (in the United States) or audit? They should also have conflict of interest and conflict of commitment policies.

6. *What kind of results have they achieved in the past?*

    Start with their website, but you also need to talk with staff and others in the field. Some areas to consider are:

    o The alignment of their mission with the way they use their resources. In the 990, the required annual tax reporting form for registered nonprofits in the U.S. charities report on their largest programs and the funding they allocate to them. You should determine whether or not the funding allocation reported seems properly aligned with what the charity says it does.

    o Whether or not they have a clear logic for achieving results. Do they explain the problem they address and how they achieve results? Does their statement of how they work seem plausible and reasonable? Do they show evidence that their approach is effective?

    o Has the charity's approach been reviewed by an objective third party? Have they made the results of this third-party analysis available publicly?

Also, tune into the news; see what recent media coverage says about them. Have they been involved in any questionable practices? You don't want anything to come back to reflect negatively on your company or strategy further down the line.

Answering these six questions will reassure you they're the kind of organization that can deliver results and that you'll be proud to introduce as a partner.

Notes from the Field

The Strategic Giving Test

Kate Rubin is Managing Director, North American Operations for eRevalue. She retired as Vice President of Social Responsibility and President of the Foundation at United Health Group

Corporate and Foundation Giving Programs need to be strategic. You've heard that many times, and read it in this guide. So what does that mean and how do you do it? Here are a few key lessons I've learned.

Strategic means Aligned — around mission and vision and how you go about getting results. It needs to be broad enough to include many opportunities, but narrow enough that you "can't drive a MACK truck through it." In my work, mission was ultimately targeted at HEALTH, aligned with a corporate citizenship mission of "Helping Build Healthier Communities," with specified focus areas. This aligned well with the corporate mission of "Helping People Live Healthier Lives," yet provided a community-based approach for grants and partnerships.

Strategic means Clear Responsibility and Accountability — We started with national giving coming from both the Foundation and the Corporation, including separate boards, committees, and processes for these as well as another committee for Corporate Home Town giving, and separate processes for each of the seven business units. Ultimately, we moved from five decision-making boards to two, consisting of the same individuals, and board meetings were held back-to-back on the same day. One board considered Foundation requests, and the other considered business requests that would have been inappropriate for the Foundation to fund.

Individual business unit requests followed a similar "delegation of authority" process, whereby lower level dollar requests could be approved within the business, but larger requests (limits should be set based on overall enterprise giving) must come to the corporate committee for approval, to ensure alignment and prevent duplication across the enterprise.

Strategic means Clear, Easy to Understand Processes — This benefits both nonprofit partners and enterprise employees. Transitioning from an *ad hoc* process where proposals from potential partners were considered as they approached colleagues at various times, to a clearly defined, once or twice a year Request for Proposals process focused on key target areas and geographies was a positive step in bringing strategic alignment. It also helped with time management!

Engaging enterprise business leaders, beginning with identification of strong nonprofits in their geography, and as "eyes and ears on the ground" was helpful in getting the anticipated outcomes, and providing guidance as well as an early warning if projects were off track. It was also a terrific way to engage employees in volunteer efforts, which ultimately creates even more impact.

GIFTS DRIVEN BY RECIPROCITY

Some corporate gifts are driven by business relationships. In the United States especially, this is an expected form of business relationship reciprocity. Service providers are often asked by their clients to support charitable events, and retailers and other merchants may ask their suppliers to partner with them to support charitable causes.

However, for your primary programs there must be a strong connection to the cause among your employees. Take the example of the mutual funding of a gala dinner table. If only a few people in the company interact with the cause, the result (as you may already have observed) is corporate names on empty tables. So instead of doing that, think first if you really need to attend a charity gala dinner (many nonprofits are actually moving away from them as the overhead is often high), or if you can donate the table or give in another way. If you feel you must buy a table, consider using the event as an employee leadership development opportunity. If it's for an educational institution, invite students. Be creative. In our work with various companies we see the savviest executives filling gala tables with high-potential team members who are being evaluated for how they perform in that social environment as part of their job performance. If they need etiquette coaching or better networking skills in order to maximize those events as business development opportunities, it's very easy for their managers to see that and support them. On the other hand, consider if you could offer an event like this as a perk for staff who've been spectacular volunteers during the year.

MANAGING AND MEASURING YOUR DIVERSE PORTFOLIO

It's much easier to measure the results of your corporate giving program if you're working with a small number of larger philanthropic commitments, than a myriad of smaller ones. Why? Because it's more difficult to measure the effects of many small transactions than a couple of large ones. However, in reality it's more than likely you're going to be working with both large and small gifts and grants. The reason for this is that the strategic purpose of many of the small transactions is to develop a relationship with your employees, through supporting the causes they feel strongly about. The intensive, strategic work will be with the larger initiatives that are based on your business strategy. The key thing in either case is to develop measures that connect to the purpose of each type of giving.

For example, if your company has 5000 employees and 2000 of them are giving (and having their contributions matched) an average of $150 to charity, you can't realistically measure the impact of all those small gifts on the organizations concerned. What you can do is measure whether these employees are more engaged and have a more favorable attitude toward your company. Do you have a better word of mouth for corporate citizenship programs? Do these employees refer others to the charity? Your measures should be focused on your employees, not on the external cause.

When should you measure social impact? This can be tricky. If you're working toward specific social impact goals, you'll likely need a nonprofit partner to help you measure the outcomes that indicate progress toward your goals. If measuring progress is important to you, you'll have to be prepared to pay for assessment as part of the project. Smaller charities usually don't have the resources to provide detailed assessment data unless it's a budgeted part of your project with them. Even larger organizations can't be expected to provide outcomes data for a grant of under $50,000 (BCCCC surveys of corporate giving professionals tell us that the average corporate grant is around $25,000), unless it's data they're already collecting.

The average number of transactions per year for a company giving $10,000,000 is around 1,000. Think about how many measurement goals you could reasonably attach to this number of gifts, and what the measures should be. You can see how this presents a management challenge; we'll provide some potential solutions later in this chapter.

THE VALUE OF EMPLOYEE VOLUNTEER PROGRAMS

With longer working hours and shorter tenures, it's more difficult than ever to keep employees engaged with their jobs. The Gallup *State of the Global Workplace* study describes engaged employees as people who are psychologically committed to their jobs, and likely to be making a positive contribution to their organizations.

In that study, they found that globally a staggering 87 percent of employees are disengaged from their jobs; in the United States this hovers around 70 percent. Gallup puts disengaged employees into two groups: those who are just getting by, and those who are actually trying to undermine their company's efforts. This latter group made up 18 percent of U.S. employees at the time of the study.

Gallup also estimates actively disengaged employees cost U.S. businesses $450–$550 billion per year in productivity losses. Turnover costs are one of the major contributors to these losses, and represent on average 12 percent of a company's pre-tax income due to lost productivity, overtime, contractor fees, hiring, and onboarding costs.

However, for firms with high levels of employee engagement there are multitude of benefits[5]:

- *Financial*: higher earnings per share, 22 percent higher profitability, 25–65 percent lower turnover, and 28 percent less staff theft.

- *Stakeholder relations*: 10 percent higher customer engagement.

- *Employee performance*: 21 percent higher productivity and 37 percent less absenteeism.

- *Employee safety*: 48 percent fewer employee safety incidents.

In the Boston College Center for Corporate Citizenship's *Corporate Community Involvement Study 2015*, more than 90 percent of companies identified increased employee engagement as one of the top three benefits of their volunteer programs. Sixty percent of companies with volunteer programs evaluate the relationship between employee volunteer programs and employee engagement. Close to 90 percent of companies that measure the correlation between on-the-job volunteering and employee engagement found a positive correlation between employee participation in these programs and employee engagement scores. This demonstrates that employees who participate in corporate volunteering report higher commitment and loyalty to their company than their peers who do not. Many companies also believe that engagement, done right, should also drive business value vectors as innovation, productivity and retention of high-performing employees. Some progressive employers are seeking to measure and manage this dynamic of engagement as well.

Employees May be More Motivated by the Opportunity to Do Well Than to Do Good

According to a 2008 study,[6] while the desire to do good in the community may be the reason many employees decide to volunteer *outside* of work it's not what drives them to participate in corporate volunteer programs. Instead, many are drawn by skill development and networking opportunities. Think about how you can you harness this for your program.

Both private and public recognition can increase volunteerism, according to a 2013 study;[7] companies that recognize exemplary employees are more likely to report success with employee volunteer participation. This can include recognition through external platforms such as local or national news, awards, or a combination of both. Companies recognizing their employees report an average employee participation rate of 41 percent, compared to 23 percent for companies that do not offer recognition. What's more, employee volunteer programs, particularly for those that are strategic and engage employees through recognition, can help companies increase employee engagement and ultimately reduce the costs detailed above.

Amplifying Employee Efforts as Part of Your Company's Commitment to the Community

Companies clearly recognize the value of employee volunteer programs in attracting prospective employees, as well as retaining their current workforce. Nearly 60 percent of companies include information about their volunteer programs during employee recruitment,[8] which is consistent with recent research that found prospective employees were more drawn to a company when their corporate citizenship efforts were illustrated in their corporate materials.

To communicate volunteer efforts effectively, you need to think about how to engage employees at different stages in their careers. While only 9 percent of companies consider the opportunity to identify future leaders as a top benefit of employee volunteer programs, research finds employees in the earlier stages of their careers (aged 18–39) are most motivated by career development and promotion opportunities. Older employees (aged 55 to 66 and over), however, are most deeply engaged by supervisor support and recognition.[9] Moreover, in the Corporation for National and Community Service's *2014 Volunteering and Civic Engagement in the United States* report, people between 35 and 44 were most likely to volunteer, closely followed by those between 45 and 54.

You can also make use of employee volunteering in your company's team-building and development. Almost 80 percent of organizations offer volunteer programs to managers to help them develop their teams, and more than 20 percent[10] of companies that offer volunteer programs also incorporate volunteer participation feedback within their employee performance reviews. Ten percent even provide financial incentives for participation.

Business executives and corporate citizenship professionals clearly agree: community involvement contributes to reputational and employee-related business goals. In the Boston College Center for Corporate Citizenship's *State of Corporate Citizenship 2014* survey, the majority of executives across all industries reported community involvement contributed to overall company success. The study also reveals it even contributes to business goals that aren't directly or obviously related to corporate giving or employee volunteering. For example, half of energy companies say community involvement helps improve risk management, while more than half of food companies report it contributes to securing a sustainable supply chain.

Organizing employees to volunteer and support these issues can be a great way to amplify the effects of your cash gifts, raise awareness for the cause your company is committed to, and develop skills and goodwill among your employees.

MAKE IT EASIER

If you're struggling with how to carve out more time to assess results or move to larger giving partnerships, you might be able to make operational enhancements that can streamline giving. Are many of your requests *ad hoc*? Consider moving to a request schedule, either quarterly or semi-annually, that allows you breathing space the rest of the year so you can evaluate programs, visit sites, and other work that's focused on strategic outcomes. Think about it — if you're handling requests across the course of the year, you're spending 80 percent of your time processing transactions, and that's not a strategic activity. Many companies have evolved their giving to one or two grant cycles a year, and even avoid the grant request cycle completely by proactively seeking out strategic nonprofits to support. There are also extensive technology tools to help you and your company manage the tracking, grant-making, and results reporting for your corporate giving programs.

LEGACY RELATIONSHIPS

If you're like most corporations, you manage a diverse portfolio of giving, and several of these are bound to remain for historical reasons. Maybe your company supports the local Boys and Girls Club because it's done so for 100 years, and to move away from that because it doesn't fit with the company strategy would be sending the wrong message. It can be tempting to ignore measurement in these cases, as you can't really justify this activity for any strategic or financial reason, but it's just as important to be visible on your reporting for these programs as it is for strategic programs. Only by being public and clear on the costs are you able to discuss the benefits to the company and the community, and determine if you could be doing more good with your strategic program elsewhere.

In terms of measuring your activities (we've talked about this in more detail in previous chapters) it's worth mentioning here too. We regularly speak with companies who give away millions of dollars a year, with no idea whether what they're doing is making a difference either externally or internally. Don't let that be you. Measurement and evaluation are critical for managing your community involvement efforts, as they give you a systematic way of identifying, collecting and analyzing data you can use to improve the performance of your partnership. Although evaluation usually happens at the end of the program, you need to consider how you're going to do it right from the beginning. Refer to Chapter 4 to refresh your knowledge on designing for measurement and beginning with the end in mind.

WHAT WE'VE COVERED

- Your corporate giving program is an extension of your corporate citizenship strategy.

- There are two elements to your corporate giving program, both of which are equally valid:

  - Your strategic support of nonprofits to support your overall business strategy.

  - Your tactical support of charities which your employees favor, as a way to increase employee engagement.

- For most companies, there's no need to set up a foundation in order to give to nonprofit causes

- There are six key questions to ask yourself when choosing a nonprofit partner. These questions are based on strategic fit, the amount you want to give and how you would like to give it, and the credibility of the organization in question.

- Try to limit exposure and do not constantly evaluate new charitable requests as they arise; instead set up a regular cycle of assessment.

- Measurement is essential, whether for strategic or tactical projects.

QUESTIONS TO ANSWER BEFORE YOU MOVE ON

1. Have you defined the core focus and strategic intent of your corporate giving? Can you describe what you are trying to deliver succinctly — to your business and to your community?

2. Have you decided what the balance should be between strategic (company strategy related) giving, and tactical (employee engagement) giving?

3. Can you describe the parts of your corporate giving strategy that support core strategic causes, employee engagement, community needs, and those informed by other drivers (such as legacy, reciprocal arrangements, and causes mandated by executives)?

4. Do you or will you leverage a Corporate Foundation or Corporate Giving strategy or a combination of both?

5. Do you know which causes your company is already donating to or investing in, and why?

6. Do you have records of what's been donated in the past, and the measurement of results from these donations?

7. Have you identified a set of prospective new partners, based on the six criteria provided in this chapter?

8. Do you have measurement plans and agreements in place?

9. Do you have reporting and communication mechanisms to leverage results with employees, communities, and external stakeholders?

10. What is the unique or differentiating aspect of your corporate giving strategy when compared with your sector, competition, or geographic peers?

NOTES

1. The Boston College Center for Corporate Citizenship (2015).

2. Grant, Dutton, and Rosso (2008).

3. Gallup (2013).

4. Becker-Olsen (2006), The Boston College Center for Corporate Citizenship (2014), Jones, Willness, and Madey (2014).

5. Jones (2010) and Jones et al. (2014).

6. The Boston College Center for Corporate Citizenship (2015).

7. Winterich, Mittal, and Aquino (2013).

8. The Boston College Center for Corporate Citizenship (2015).

9. Boone, McKechnie, and Swanberg (2011).

10. The Boston College Center for Corporate Citizenship (2015).

SECTION 3

PULLING IT ALL TOGETHER

9

IF A SUSTAINABLY HARVESTED TREE FALLS IN THE FOREST AND THERE IS NO ONE THERE TO HEAR IT ... GETTING YOUR MESSAGE ACROSS

It's clear by now that the way to achieve success in corporate citizenship is by working with and through other people. Solo players are seldom successful. Communicating with others persuasively and effectively is absolutely pivotal to the success of your program. We're often asked by new entrants to the field or those trying to get their first corporate citizenship roles, "what is the most important skill needed to be successful in corporate citizenship?" We agree that the answer to that question is — excellent communication skills. Multiple research studies prove, time and again, that communication is a necessary ingredient to deliver maximum social and business value from your company's corporate citizenship investments.[1] Without increasing awareness to build support and report results, even your best plans will fail to deliver.

This means your messages in all channels and to all audiences need to be crystal clear: simple, limited, truthful, incorporating both values and facts. Ideally they should also include a call to action.

Why a call to action? Because all corporate citizenship work is about *change*. To get people on board with your envisioned transformation, you must let them know what it is you want them to do — and even more importantly, what the opportunity is to make things better. Your work is not about preserving the status quo. You want to protect and build your company's reputation while you create more business and social value. By the very nature of that aspiration, you need to move people from where they are today to someplace new: a more desirable future state for both your business and society.

If you're like most corporate citizenship professionals, you're probably not a trained communications expert, and that's fine because this chapter is designed to help you become more skilled and focused with your messages.

The biggest mistake people make when they're trying to get people on their side is to assume what's important to them (the communicator) is also important to their audience. Not as a matter of judgment, but as a matter of fact, this is simply not true most of the time. Your internal and external audiences have many things on their minds other than your corporate citizenship program; they have jobs to do, bosses to keep happy, families to feed, and friends to spend time with. So when you communicate with them, you want to identify and address the issues that are most important to *them*, keeping in mind that those things may be different from what is top-of-mind for you. In other words, it's not about what you *need* to say, it's about what they *are able* to hear and the actions they *want* to take.

Earlier we introduced what has become a well-known acronym — WIIFM, or "what's in it for me?" Think of WIIFM as being the information channel everybody likes to tune into. You need to tune yourself in to that channel if you want your audience's attention. The next time you send out a corporate communication, look at what you've written and see if you can easily answer the question "what's in it for me?" from your readers' perspectives. If you can't, it's a guarantee most of them will be sending it to the recycle bin as soon as they receive it.

Notes from the Field

2-Way Communication Drives Program Development

Lori Forte Harnick is Chief Operating Officer of Microsoft Philanthropies

Microsoft's mission is to empower every person and every organization on the planet to achieve more. This mission is more than a statement: it is the North Star for how the company runs its business, how it serves its customers, and how it engages in its communities around the world.

Microsoft Philanthropies is a dedicated team within the company that plays an important role in bringing this mission to life. The commercial technology ecosystem, while incredibly important and impactful, does not fully meet the needs of all people and organizations around the world. We must create opportunity in society to reach the widest possible segment of the global population.

As Microsoft Philanthropies pursues this goal, it creates value for both society and the company. Because it sits inside the company, Microsoft Philanthropies is able to leverage the three greatest assets the company offers — its technology, its talent, and its voice — to do the greatest good across a strong foundation of community investments and partnerships around the world.

This is more important now than ever as we enter the "Fourth Industrial Revolution" and digital transformation sweeps across industries and economies worldwide. To bring the benefits of technology closer to those who need them most, Microsoft Philanthropies donates, through its Tech for Good program, $1 billion of the company's software and services to more than 100,000 nonprofit organizations each year. Not only do we offer solutions, but we also listen and collect intelligence from our partner organizations and community members about what they need. This has led us to develop our programs in several directions.

We've learned that the value for nonprofits is not only in improvement of their "back-office" processes and functions, but also in access to new tools and services that help nonprofits better serve their communities, better engage with their donors, and better report their results.

One insight we've gathered from this program is that nonprofits frequently need talent to help them make the most of the donated technology. This has spurred Microsoft Philanthropies to build a skills-based volunteering program.

We've also found that we can use our voice to draw attention to the challenges — and solutions — of today's pressing issues. Through Microsoft Philanthropies, we've created a number of new social good marketing initiatives that shine a spotlight on issues in local and global communities and provide an opportunity for public engagement and action while also delivering on the promise of our mission and brand. Recent examples include encouraging girls to study math and science through www.makewhatsnext.com and supporting the missions of 100+ nonprofit organizations through Upgrade Your World.

Additionally, you need to communicate consistently and often. It can be hard to believe, but people need to read, see, or hear a message at least 3−5 times on average in order to recall it. So when you can't stand to hear yourself say something once more, it's probably the first moment your audience really hears it. You need to keep repeating! Those busy lives we talked about earlier mean their attention is usually far from your cause; it takes a lot of repetition for even a simple statement to move from awareness to action.

This gap between your audience's daily experience and your own can lead to what we call "the curse of knowledge." All the hard work you've put into your corporate citizenship program means you're an expert, and it's easy to forget your audience doesn't have that same advantage. So think about using simple language, speak in their terms, to fully explain the concepts. Speak to their level of understanding about the change you're trying to create. Questions your communication should answer for listeners might include:

- *What?* What's the key idea you're trying to communicate (in words a fourth grader could understand)?

- *So what?* Why is this issue important?

- *What does it mean to me?* How are you addressing audience concerns?

- *Now what?* What do you want them to do?

Years ago, corporate communication was more straightforward. All you had to do was create a press release, book some press slots, maybe create a publicity campaign, and your message would be delivered intact in a predictable way. Now with the advent of digital and social communication, it's far from simple. The number of channels has increased exponentially and people expect to be communicated with on a much more individualized basis than ever before. They also expect communication to be two-way, not just one-way. Different segments of your audience will have different concerns so your communications can't be a one-size-fits-all. Customers will have interests that are distinct from those of employees; junior staff will have different priorities than the CEO or your managerial colleagues. Investors, policy makers, local partners, and topical trend leaders will each have different priorities and therefore their own place in your communications strategy.

HOW TO CREATE A COMPELLING CALL TO ACTION

There are several great books on the topics of influence and the key principles of psychology, which will help you create persuasive communications for your stakeholders. Whether you refer to Robert B. Cialdini's *The Psychology of Influence*, Heath and Heath's *Made to Stick* (one of Dave's particular favorites),

Frank Luntz's *Words that Work*, or Malcolm Gladwell's *The Tipping Point*, you'll find they share common principles about what constitutes persuasive communication. You can put these to good use when you're managing your relationships with both internal and external audiences. Here's a construct we've developed that leverages elements of all four; it can help you to remember all the functional attributes you should be trying to build into your communications. A good message T-R-A-V-E-L-S.

Time sensitive: the most effective communications have time boundaries. We find things more attractive when their availability is limited, or when we stand to lose an opportunity if we don't act. The fear of losing out is a powerful motivation that drives people to mobilize in response to messages that employ the tactic; this is popularly called FOMO, the "fear of missing out." For instance, we might buy something if we're told it's the last one, or that a special offer will expire soon. If you can make your communications and appeals time-bound you're likely to have greater success in getting people on board with your requests. Creating a deadline for expressions of interest in your program could work well to activate this part of our human nature.

Rational: human beings have a deep desire to be consistent. Although we often respond to the emotional elements of appeals, our minds will work hard to justify why this would be a good decision. For this reason, once we've made a first, small commitment to something, we're more likely to take a larger next step which is consistent with it. This means giving your audience opportunities to rationalize their commitment is a good tactic. For instance, you'd be more inclined to support a colleague's project if you'd shown an interest in it when he first talked to you, or to serve on a task force after you'd already been invited to review a document outlining the scope of the work.

Humans like to think they are rational and prefer to respond to facts (even when we are not doing so). So use specifics in your communications; these lend credibility to the rational evaluation of your message by your audience, especially when you want to prove larger assertions.

Context is important here, too. Focusing on the proportion of children who don't get breakfast at home (1 in 10) means more to people than simply giving the total number of children; the relationships between numbers are often more important than absolute values because they help to describe the context and magnitude of issues.

Action-oriented: remember, corporate citizenship is ultimately about driving change. Your intention is to continually improve your company's ESG performance and the world in which you live; these are huge goals that require influence far beyond the reach of your individual audience members. If your "ask" is too ambitious, they'll file the action under "maybe later, when I've retired"; instead, try to make it something they can do right now, today.

Validating: as humans we tend to be hyper aware of what other people in our group are doing. When we were cave dwellers, we looked to the behavior of the herd to stay safe; now this is how we establish norms, which is basically another way of staying safe. Two tactics you can use to activate validation are safety in numbers and authority.

If your communication establishes that "everyone is doing it," you're more likely to persuade others to participate, especially if the "everyone" is a group your audience feels an affinity with. You can establish affinity and identification in multiple ways. We often seek validation from people we like, and likability comes in many forms: people similar to or familiar to us, people who've given us compliments, or people who are magnetic or attractive. You can activate this principle by creating communications that acknowledge the values of the listeners and in a tone that's welcoming to the people you want to get on board.

You can activate the idea of authority in a number of ways as well. If your boss is involved and it's clear your corporate citizenship program is important to him or her, others are more likely to get involved. Job titles, uniforms, and even gadgets can lend an air of authority. For you, your in-depth knowledge about the company and its community can be a source of authority. Authority is also something that can be conferred; you can create and then reinforce the authority of others in your communications, by identifying them as expert resources for instance.

Emotional: although people want to be logical in their decisions, research tells us time and again that we're tremendously influenced by emotion. We tend to recall the way a communication made us feel more easily than its actual substance. This is because emotions are a form of disruption to our usual state. They move us out of equilibrium into a state of arousal that requires a different way of engaging with the world. This means more of our brain is involved with the communication we're experiencing, which in turn helps us to remember it. People are also more likely to spend more time with communications that surprise them or leave questions unanswered. In a now well-known study, researchers sent a letter requesting a group of psychologists take an action; half of them got the full letter that included a call to action in the conclusion, and the other half got only the first page that ended with a dangling clause. The recipients who only got the half letter responded to the experimenters in far greater numbers than those who got the full call to action. Their feelings of surprise and discomfort at not having the full picture motivated them to act. There's a well-documented psychological reason for this; if everything seems normal we don't pay much attention, but the minute we experience disruption to our understanding of the world we become alert.

You can also activate your audience's feelings toward others in order to increase the persuasiveness of your messages. We are social beings and tend to want to treat others as they treat us. This can lead us to feel that we must help other people if they have helped us. The key to success in employing this tactic is to be the first to give, and also to personalize your giving to the recipient.

Humor can be an incredibly important emotion to get people to pay attention to your message. Think about the Ice Bucket Challenge; the power of this was in the delight we got from seeing the CEO get into his skivvies and throw water over himself. We love to see the humanity in people, and laughter is something we all share. So pulling on the heartstrings is important, and humor is often what seals the deal.

How does this help your communications? By employing a range of emotions — from outrage to humor — and by including an element of unexpectedness, you can make them much more memorable.

Limited: this element is critical in the age of digital technology. Think 140 characters, 2.5 by 3 inches, and visual. The first is the number of characters allowed by Twitter, the second is the average screen real estate on a mobile screen, and the last is the attribute that will make your message much more likely to be opened. Communications are not something we sit down to receive; we process them 24/7. Recent research from the Pew Trust tells us the average American receives more than 3000 messages across all channels in any given day. Combine this with the fact that 55 percent of people need to hear something between three and five times before they can recall it, and another 20 percent need to hear it as many as 10 times.[2] These two points taken together underscore the importance of limiting your communications to only the most salient points. You should be able to capture your core message in 25 words or less, offering richer explorations to your audience as they become more engaged with your content.

Simple: recall and repetition go hand in hand. Try to write your message in a way so anyone can understand it. Your audience doesn't know everything you do, nor do they need to, so keep your communications at their level. Clear, uncluttered statements repeated over time will have a dramatic effect. You can simplify things by staying focused on what your message means for a specific audience member. If your communication is for a mass audience, think of the motivations that speak to each group. For example: "for our leadership this is a staff development tool, for our company this is a way to integrate with our community, for our employees this is a way to add interest to their jobs, and for our communities this is an essential health improvement initiative."

Remember: elementary language, short sentences, and vivid images work well.

CATHEDRAL THINKING

Cathedral thinking[3] is a term used to describe the act of envisioning, and then getting others to share and act upon a vision for the future. If you cast your mind back to your history lessons, you'll remember the Middle Ages was the golden era of cathedral building in Europe. As you can imagine, creating these amazing places of worship was no simple matter and not only because of the painstaking work involved. With the rise of the trades, skilled artisans were becoming mobile and able to demand to be paid in currency; this meant they were free to sell their services to the highest bidder. So community leaders needed to inspire these workers to commit to the project by creating vivid images of what the future was destined to be.

Their extra challenge was that because a cathedral took decades to build, some workers would never see the end results of their labors; they could only trust that by the time their grandchildren were born the work might be approaching completion. Those who were sponsoring these massive edifices that took generations to build were not only building structures, they were building real and symbolic monuments to ideals important to their society. These were buildings that communicated big ideas and served big purposes. So their communications weren't only aimed at the individual workers who started the job, they were also targeted toward the successive generations who had to continue the building process. They had to inspire them about the functional, social, and emotional benefits involved. On a functional level, they were paid to do the work; on a social level they were part of the craft community; and on an emotional level they were in service to the greater glory of their God and the nobility who funded the projects. You can see how, from the time of the inception of Western civilization, we've activated these different motivations in people in order to get the best out of them.

So what are your cathedrals? They're the vivid images of how things will be different if your corporate citizenship initiative works out as you intend. How can you make your audience understand what that will mean to your communities and to their business enterprises, now and tomorrow? Do you know what success looks like? How will your workplace, community, and marketplace be different once you've achieved it: what will it look and feel like to them? Can you describe it succinctly to each of your audiences in their language, in a way that helps them see the benefits, and with visual images that trigger an emotional response? What details would bring it to life?

Being able to describe what success looks and feels like is critical to every change management strategy, whether you're the CEO or an intern. Test it out in your own communications and challenge others to do the same.

Emotions come from the vision you paint for your audience. Have you helped them to imagine a world in which all children achieve to their best potential because they've eaten a healthy breakfast? What would it be like for every family to sit down to a nourishing, home-cooked meal at night because the parents have the skills to cook? Get people excited about the potential, about what can be achieved. Dig into your own emotions so you can convey them to your audience. What did you feel the first time you visited the new breakfast club and talked to the kids? Can you show pictures of them enjoying their food and running around at school?

WHAT WE'VE COVERED

- Good communication is pivotal to your success as a corporate citizenship professional.

- Always think, "What's in it for me?" as you prepare communications for various audiences.

- Your communications shouldn't be a one-size-fits-all effort; they need to be tailored to your individual audiences.

- There are various facets of human nature, which you can use to persuasive effect. Remember a well-planned message TRAVELS:
  o Time sensitive

  o Rational

  o Action-oriented

  o Validating

  o Emotional

  o Limited

  o Simple

10 QUESTIONS TO ANSWER BEFORE YOU MOVE ON

1. Have you done an audit of all your current corporate citizenship communications, so you know what goes out when, and to whom?

2. Do they live up to the standards we went through in this chapter?

3. If not, have you worked out how to address this going forward?

4. Have you created a strong working partnership with your corporate communications team? Who is your primary connection? Have you discussed the cadence of internal and external communications as a team?

5. The next time you create a communication, have you worked out the WIIFM?

6. Have you identified your main audiences so you know who they are and what you want them to do with the information you're sharing?

7. What are the key functional, social, and emotional needs of each?

8. Do you understand the key elements of human nature, which effect how we absorb communications?

9. Can you create some vivid and emotional stories that will help your audience feel more involved with what you do?

10. Can you describe what success looks and feels like in a business and a social context?

NOTES

1. Margolis, Elfenbein, and Walsh (2007).

2. Edelman (2013).

3. Cathedral Thinking, concept first introduced by former Duke Energy Chairman and CEO James E. Rogers in Zakaria (2007).

10

BUILDING ON YOUR SUCCESS

You've come a long way, haven't you? You've defined your purpose, you've created your strategy, and now you understand how corporate citizenship has the potential to transform your company at every level. In the process, you've looked at all the opportunities available to you, from your supply chain to how consumers view and interact with your company's products. You've also discovered tools to help track and implement all the changes you'll be making, so your work is organized, well communicated, recognized, and respected throughout your organization.

The next step is for you to ensure your strategies systematically evolve and improve over time, which means developing management systems and reporting structures capable of being interpreted by anyone who wants to understand your company's corporate citizenship performance. This is important because if you do this correctly, others will use your reporting not only to communicate the results you've achieved, but also to manage future performance. Imagine what a shame it would be if the improvements you put in place were to decline over the years. You are only one person, after all, and you're not going to be in the same position forever. With the knowledge you've gained from this book you're going to be in hot demand as a corporate citizenship professional elsewhere before too long or you'll be tapped to help lead new projects within your organization. This chapter is about how you ensure your methods for executing your strategy include performance assessment and continuity plans, with the result that your firm's corporate citizenship will continue to improve and you'll leave a system in place that helps it to excel for years to come.

USING EXTERNAL REPORTING AND DISCLOSURE TO YOUR ADVANTAGE

Reporting is a labor-intensive process. At times it may feel like the least glamorous part of your job, but you can't be a successful corporate citizenship professional without understanding the key reporting frameworks. All businesses are seeking structured ways to communicate their corporate citizenship strategy and performance; if you're not doing this yet, you can bet you're being expected to do so by your community, your shareowners, and other stakeholders such as policy makers and regulators. You really can't ignore this area. Having said that, you can leverage your reporting process to drive even better results. The time you spend generating reports should never be written off as administration, because the process of reporting is a powerful tool in its own right.

Reporting and disclosure are integral to your long-term success as a corporate citizenship professional. Of course, reporting is nothing new; companies have been managing and disclosing performance metrics in one way or another for decades. What has changed recently is broader groups of stakeholders are now demanding increasing amounts of information about corporate performance way beyond financial boundaries. There are a number of reporting standards and guidelines that are global drivers for this; we won't cover them all, but we'll help you understand how the main ones work and their impact on you.

Notes from the Field

. . . .

How Reporting Can Help Improve the Management of Environmental and Social Impact

Rick Pearl is Vice President and Global Corporate Responsibility Officer at State Street

External influences, such as client or shareholder questions or pressure from competitors, often influence a company's decision to report on its environmental, social and corporate governance (ESG) efforts. Once they begin the corporate responsibility reporting process, they may be happy to find there are efficiencies and lessons learned that can help improve operations.

At State Street, we began ESG reporting in 2003 after we received a request for environmental information from a European ESG stock index. That inquiry added to a growing awareness that our company's corporate citizenship profile had extended to include more than just charitable contributions and volunteer hours. As a result, the company's annual community report was expanded to include some basic, Scope 1 environmental data, including CO_2 emissions from direct energy (oil and gas for HVAC) usage in its Massachusetts' headquarter facilities.

For us, corporate responsibility reporting has become an annual exercise in determining the most relevant information to provide to our external stakeholders. We work with internal stakeholders to collect, analyze, and benchmark data, and then write, review, and audit our report and post it on our website in time for our annual shareholders' meeting. This has helped cast a spotlight on areas of our company where we could improve corporate responsibility. As a result, each reporting year has led to unique lessons learned and enhancements to various processes.

Gathering new and different ESG information has also helped us prepare for timely responses to new legislative or client requirements on environmental and social issues across our global locations. As an example, in building our environmental program, we enhanced our environmental management system (EMS) based on ISO 14001 specs. We were bidding on a contract to service a large European public pension scheme and one of the requirements was ISO certification at the bidders' facilities. It was a natural next step to have our EMS certified and it ultimately helped us to win the contract. On the legislative side, a social issue — slavery and human trafficking — has become a regulatory concern in several jurisdictions, including the United States. Work done over the years with the human resources, procurement and legal departments to answer questions about these issues for the CR Report helped lead to enhanced policies and programs in this area.

External demands may always be an impetus to report on ESG factors, but the opportunities from a thorough review of the policies and programs supporting a more responsible approach to corporate citizenship should not be overlooked. In many ways, it makes the additional expense and time devoted to a strong corporate responsibility report well worth it.

Many of these reporting standards and guidelines organizations are working to become aligned with each other. With consistent reports, interested parties can see which companies are doing best in corporate citizenship within a sector, or even across sectors, and then decide where to invest their money or amplify the most authentic stories. The value of a reporting standard is it allows stakeholders to understand how organizations are performing on multiple dimensions in an "apples to apples" kind of way, providing a common language across international boundaries for understanding ESG performance. What's more, standards and guidelines for reporting have even evolved to the point where it's now an established industry.

The first and most widely known of these reporting frameworks was developed by a group known as CERES (the Coalition for Environmentally Responsible Economies). CERES created a global reporting framework in 1997 called the Global Reporting Initiative (GRI). This changed the landscape for corporate citizenship reporting forever, with the result that the GRI evolved into a stand-alone influential organization in its own right. The United Nations, for instance, has adopted the GRI reporting standard, and GRI has developed sector-specific reporting guidelines for areas such as utilities, financial services, oil and gas, and even food processing. Thousands of European companies have adopted the GRI standard, and 95 percent of the 250 largest global companies use it. GRI's reporting framework is now in its fourth generation, commonly known as G4 and is headed toward becoming a set of topical standards. If you work for a large publicly traded company you may already be familiar with it, but even if you're not it's important to understand a bit about what the G4 reporting framework consists of.

We could write an entire book just on this subject; in full disclosure, the Boston College Center for Corporate Citizenship is a certified training partner of GRI, the International Integrated Reporting Committee (IIRC), and the CDP. All the major accounting firms around the world, and thousands of consultancies, have services to help companies compile these types of reports and assure some of the data. Building the capacity internally for this — even just to follow the GRI standard — is a significant investment, especially if you're doing it for the first time.

GRI may be the most common, globally adopted reporting standard but it's not the only one; there's a different reporting structure for almost every sector, running into hundreds overall. Different than GRI, but related in many ways and broadly adopted, is the CDP. Started in 2000, it gradually evolved from a few voluntary questions for companies to answer about climate change policy and practice, to the comprehensive set of surveys it is today. More than 3000 companies now participate annually. CDP also manages other extensive disclosure requests, and reports not just on climate change but also on supply chain, performance and operations, water disclosure, forest and fiber disclosure — there's even a report designed for cities.

Given that these reporting standards are voluntary, you may be wondering if you need to participate. CDP publicly ranks companies based on the information it receives. Major players such as Walmart, Dell, and PepsiCo use it as a way of ensuring sustainability within their supply chains; they actually send the report to their suppliers and insist it's filled out so they can manage compliance through their sourcing procedures and practices. So CDP has gone from being a small assessment tool to being part of the corporate reporting infrastructure used by investors and companies themselves to manage environmental impacts throughout the value chain.

How can you best tackle this reporting challenge? Your first step is to spend a little time on the GRI website (see below), and familiarize yourself with the standards. Both GRI and CDP are large, reputable nonprofits that have a lot of resources online. After that, talk with the person in your company who manages financial reporting; in the United States the external regulatory requirement is the SEC, so whoever manages your 10K and proxy statements will be able to help. What we often see is that offices of the general counsel, who file the SEC paperwork, are actually reporting ESG risks in their disclosures in ways that differ from their corporate citizenship colleagues. To avoid this, you need to work with your disclosure and compliance team to ensure accurate and consistent ESG disclosures.

It's obviously easier if you have previous corporate citizenship reports to learn from, so use them as a starting point if possible. You can also subscribe to services that aggregate company data and reports and post their findings publicly; these will help you with your external benchmarking. Other companies' websites often show their own reporting so you may be able to check out your competitors, as well.

Here are some key websites which will help you further:

www.globalreporting.org (the GRI main website)

www.database.globalreporting.org/search (one of the public data sites we mentioned above)

www.corporateregister.com

www.ccc.bc.edu/sustainability-reporting.html (Boston College's main resource on reporting)

www.sec.gov/spotlight/disclosure-effectiveness.shtml

www.csrwire.com/reports

www.ec.europa.eu/justice/civil/company-law/eu-company-law/index_en.htm

It's worth bearing in mind that sustainability reports are mandatory in certain regions. If you're operating in global markets and are unsure about whether your company's disclosure requirements include sustainability or ESG reporting, refer to one of the websites above.

INTEGRATED REPORTING

This is a rapidly emerging trend, in which corporate citizenship reporting is increasingly being integrated into traditional financial reporting. For instance, in 2010 the U.S. SEC added guidance for climate change risk reporting for all U.S. publicly traded companies. Global stock exchanges, including those in the United States, have and will continue to integrate sustainability and corporate citizenship criteria into their listing requirements, which also has the effect of increasing standard reporting requirements. While we were working on this book, the U.S. SEC issued a request for public comments on the subject of integrating ESG topics into standard financial reporting guidelines.

Integrated reporting isn't only being driven by regulation, but also by companies who are experimenting with different ways of combining their financial and corporate citizenship disclosures. The benefit to corporations is they're able to show they're trying to improve what they're doing, by being open about where it's working and where it's not. They are effectively saying they would rather help create this and be a part of the journey, rather than let it be dictated from the outside.

In the United States, one of the more interesting integrated reporting developments is being pursued by the Sustainability Accounting Standards Board, or SASB. Their mission is to develop and disseminate sustainability accounting standards to provide decision-useful information to investors. SASB has issued sector-based disclosure standards.

While integrated reporting may be slow to develop in the United States, the trend is clear. This is something for you to watch and learn from over the next decade.

LEVERAGING YOUR REPORTS

Although you don't have to understand every nuance of each reporting framework — that would be impossible — you do need to know they exist. With all the work you'll be putting into this, it can be hard to see the payback; it can feel overwhelming. But investors, regulatory advisors, and to a certain extent your customers will increasingly be expecting companies like yours to participate in the large disclosure frameworks in the future. If you work in a publicly traded company almost anywhere in the world, you'll be included in certain investor indices and rankings whether you like it or not. More and more investment and research firms are analyzing your company, and investors are using these reports as a guide. The investment industry creates indices of the best companies in each sector or region; if you're a publicly traded company you're likely already ranked and profiled by more than one. Some of these lists are public, while others may be kept as research tools or sold to institutional investors as research intelligence.

While much analyst coverage of ESG data today is binary (the company data is either available or not available; and the company either meets or doesn't meet an internal ESG screen) and may not go as far as evaluating the quality or performance of the data, this trend is shifting. Five years ago, only socially responsible investors or SRIs (SRIs are synonymous with ESG thematic investors — those investors that employ ESG screens to investment decisions) routinely reviewed corporate citizenship performance as part of their screening process. Today, ESG considerations are common, not only for SRIs but also for large institutional investors such as pension funds and universities. These are hugely influential; it's estimated they command more than 70 percent of the $100 trillion in capital invested globally. And with influential systems such as CalPERS (California's pension and retirement fund) making ESG performance criteria part of their investment screening process, others are likely to follow.

Some of these frameworks can be viewed as guidance alone, to help you decide where to focus your efforts; you'll want to make disclosures where you have the largest potential impacts and opportunities. By approaching reporting as a mode of communication that can drive change, you'll help your company make continuous improvements. It's very difficult for executives to go backwards once they've committed, so reporting helps the company move forward by providing them with a reminder of progress toward their goals. Instead of *you* asking the difficult questions, it's effectively an *investor intermediary* doing the questioning. Executives love to listen to those with financial influence and a stake in the company's long-term success.

As such, reporting processes are also an important opportunity for you to develop more influence internally. Take the DJSI for instance; this assessment tool, managed by RobecoSAM, covers just about every corporate citizenship angle you can imagine, from the supply chain and work force, to how you carry out training and development, to environmental, social, and human rights performance. It asks questions about what you do in manufacturing, how you implement eco-efficiency, and what your community affairs programming consists of. It even covers your stakeholder engagement and corporate giving and philanthropy.

As you can imagine, completing this assessment is a significant investment of time and effort. However, survey time is also an opportunity to sit down with your network of colleagues who are involved in the many dimensions of your company's corporate citizenship, and talk with them about a number of things: what they see coming down the pike, where you can help, and how you might work together. You can be a vitally important connector in your company, so that all your firm's corporate citizenship commitments are captured in a way that allows investors to decide which companies are managing their ESG impacts and opportunities most effectively.

You can even use your rankings and ratings to generate credible PR for your corporate citizenship strategy. Suppose you've done a lot of work on improving employee engagement; if you pick the right platform and put some publicity resources behind it, you could aim to receive recognition as a great place to work.

We suggest you view reporting as closing a loop in a continuous virtuous circle; strategies lead to programs and projects, which lead to improvement, which lead to more strategies and projects. Each loop is a record of progress over time. Even if you're at the top of an index or external ranking, there will be places you are weaker than others in your sector. Finding opportunities for generating more value, and combining them with what your stakeholders are thinking, your customers are demanding, and what you want to drive internally, creates a potent force for change.

We'll be honest, reporting and disclosure can be a frustrating and time-consuming business, so make sure you use the outputs to drive improvement. Ask yourself how you can use it to incrementally improve your corporate citizenship strategy and performance.

WORKING YOURSELF OUT OF A JOB — THE POWER OF INTEGRATION

As we mentioned earlier, you're only one person; even if you have a team, you're a microscopic proportion of your whole company.

And yet you can be fundamental to the success of your business. So how do you create systems to put all your learning and developments into place in such a way as they deliver a permanent and long-term change? In other words, how do you make corporate citizenship in your business less dependent on you alone?

Many corporate citizenship professionals say, in a tongue in cheek kind of way, that they're trying to work themselves out of a job. By that they mean if all the innovation and changes they're putting into place were to continue to evolve on their own, the corporate citizenship team wouldn't be needed. In an ironic way, that's what all of us in this field are aiming to do (although it's unlikely to happen, of course).

All across your company there will be various teams charged with strategic planning in their specialist areas. As we know, people move on and change roles, so companies take care to develop systems independent of individuals. Ideally, each area will have some kind of annual or periodic process they've put in place, and part of that is to embed organizational learning into the strategic process.

You can do this too. Consider holding a meeting once a month with a different functional team to share information from investors, the DJSI, CDP, or GRI, to help them understand relevant industry trends. You can also show them where your corporate citizenship strategy fits in, and work out ways to create improvements together. This gives you opportunities to encourage your colleagues to demonstrate leadership and be recognized for driving progress. Does your HR department do something spectacular with talent development? Quote the VP of HR on the value derived from your program, or write a story about their success in one of your upcoming communications. Is your procurement manager doing something cutting edge to prevent human rights abuses in your supply chain? Work with your executive officers to have your CEO recognize their efforts in the introductory letter of your report, or in an all-hands meeting.

This is a low-cost and high-impact way to build continuous momentum. However, the main opportunity with this is to impact the systems and processes within those teams, and to integrate your strategy into them. For example, you could create a module that goes into your company's standard leadership development training; a couple of slides from you every year means you're not just informing one person in a conversation, you're having an impact on every leader who goes through that program. Another way to institutionalize this is to integrate your expectations into formal performance objectives and compensation for executives. By working with your HR team to implement this, everyone holding a position of responsibility can have a line in their objectives which details what the company thinks is important around corporate citizenship, and then they know to focus on this in their annual work plan.

A common theme throughout this book has been the power of integration. From the importance of creating a corporate citizenship program that fits with your company's purpose and strategy, to building corporate citizenship into the processes and structures of your business, and to inserting sustainability and ethical considerations into the key decision-making points that happen throughout the year — all this means your work becomes embedded instead of an optional extra. When the company's strategic planning team gets to their annual review point and proactively reaches out to you for a quick assessment of your competitors' sustainability, you'll know you're starting to make an impact.

Now you need to think about everything you've learned, and everything your company's learned, and figure out how to incorporate it into these systems. People are the key to driving corporate citizenship, but moving from people into processes is what makes your strategy stick long after you've moved on to your next assignment.

THE VALUE OF CORPORATE CITIZENSHIP

You know corporate citizenship isn't just about PR, it's about developing a strategy and program that's integrated and permanent. It's not a six-month marketing program or an advertising campaign, it's a theme running throughout your company. When your customers and consumers trust your values, they'll buy more readily from you. And when your sales increase, you're able to invest in your business more purposefully.

This is the direction that most major corporations are going long term. It is not only the definition of success in the 21st century — it is an enabler of success. In order to keep up, your corporate citizenship strategy must be fully embedded within your business purpose and strategy. You need to build excellent and trusting relationships across the board, work with the key functions to get them on your side, and communicate this with integrity and authenticity.

We've tried to provide you with the key tools to begin your journey. Now it's time for you to act. Remember, corporate citizenship always means asking other people to do their jobs differently and with more ethical awareness. Your task isn't an easy one; changing things for the better never is. And the payback? You get to do good in the world at the same time that you help increase your company's profits *and* become one of the most influential people in your organization.

That's corporate citizenship done well.

WHAT WE'VE COVERED

- Reporting and disclosure increasingly depends on conforming to standardized reporting frameworks.

- These reports are used by investors to decide whether or not to focus on or invest in your organization.

- Filling out the reports is a time-consuming and labor-intensive process, but it's essential for your company's reputation.

- You can leverage the time you spend on reports by using them as a tool to drive improvement internally.

- Creating your own systems and embedding corporate citizenship into the processes of other functions in your business is key to creating a lasting legacy of improvement.

- Integrating your work with the existing strategies and systems of your business means your program becomes larger and more permanent than any individual person could be.

10 QUESTIONS TO ANSWER BEFORE YOU MOVE ON

1. Have you decided how you'll report and disclose your corporate citizenship performance?

2. Have you assigned accountability for corporate citizenship reporting and disclosure to an individual or team?

3. Do you understand the GRI and the reporting frameworks that might apply to your business?

4. Do you understand any legally required reporting and disclosure within your sector or region?

5. Do you understand the concept of integrated reporting, and could you describe it in such a way as makes sense to your Chief Financial Officer?

6. Do you know about other major reporting and disclosure frameworks such as GRI, CDP, and IIRC, DJSI, and SASB? And do you understand the different roles these organizations and others play in the reporting and disclosure landscape?

7. Have you identified other external assessments, including investor and analyst assessments, sustainability ranking

methodologies, and "best places to work" frameworks, that already rank your company or that you could use to benchmark against?

8. Do you know what your key customers expect when it comes to corporate citizenship reporting and disclosure?

9. Have you created a process to use your reporting and disclosure information within your company to drive continuous improvement?

10. How are you using external assessments of your performance, rankings and ratings, or investor evaluations, to drive continuous improvement?

LIST OF KEY TERMS

With a growing number of companies investing in socially and environmentally sustainable practices, corporate citizenship has grown and diversified exponentially over its relatively short history. An overwhelming number of new terms and acronyms have become part of the lexicon of doing good. The following glossary gives you a quick reference guide for some of the more commonly used terms and acronyms.

Let's start with what you may call your program. Here are some of the most commonly used terms:

- Corporate Citizenship

- Corporate Social Responsibility

- Corporate Responsibility

- Responsible Leadership

- Sustainability

- Social Investment

- Environmental, Social, and Governance

Try to resist the temptation to debate what your program should be called; the semantics are less important than the fact you have a program with clearly defined goals and objectives. Pick the terms that most connect to your company's culture and intention, and then move ahead. We all know what you mean.

You need to know what the terms in this glossary mean, but they're not the most important place to focus for effective programs. Don't get distracted by the plethora of standards, frameworks, initiatives, and organizations. At the heart of your great corporate citizenship program are the issues most material to your company's business strategy and purpose. One or more of the concepts and organizations described in the glossary may be helpful to your efforts. If they are, by all means, avail yourself of their resources, but be selective.

CORPORATE CITIZENSHIP GLOSSARY

B Corp (Benefit Corporation): A title granted to companies that have been certified to meet rigorous standards of social and environmental performance, and have bylaws that take into account their impact on the environment, community, and employees.

B Lab: a nonprofit organization that offers certification to businesses to become "benefit corporations" which meet higher standards of corporate purpose, accountability, and transparency.

BoP (Base/Bottom of Pyramid): a term referring to the number of people at the base of the global economic pyramid (4 billion), whose incomes are below $3,000 in local purchasing power.

CDP (Carbon Disclosure Project): an international, not-for-profit organization offering a worldwide system for companies and cities to measure, disclose, manage, and share vital environmental information.

CFP (Corporate Financial Performance): a term referring to a company's overall financial health and ability to generate revenue.

CGI (Clinton Global Initiative): founded by former President Bill Clinton, this organization brings together global leaders to create and implement innovative solutions to the world's most pressing challenges.

CO_{2e} (Carbon Dioxide Equivalent): a measure used to compare the emissions from greenhouse gases based upon their global warming potential.

CSP (Corporate Social Performance): often used as a synonym for corporate social responsibility (CSR), CSP refers to a company's interaction with the community on economic, environmental, and social issues.

CSR (Corporate Social Responsibility): efforts by businesses to work with stakeholders to achieve improved economic, environmental, and social performance, sometimes known as the triple bottom line but also identified as corporate citizenship or sustainability.

CVC (Corporate Volunteer Council): local networks for companies to share effective practices and address community needs through workplace volunteering, many of which are affiliated with local community-based agencies (HandsOn Network, Volunteer Centers, and United Way).

DJSI (Dow Jones Sustainability Index): a family of indices managed by RobecoSam Indices and S&P Dow Jones that track the stock performance of companies according to economic, environmental, and social criteria, offering a measurement by which investors can judge the sustainability impact of their investment choices.

EHS (Environmental, Health and Safety): a traditional name for departments in organizations responsible for implementing and managing environmental and occupational health and safety programs.

EICC (Electronic Industry Citizenship Coalition): a partnership of the world's leading electronics companies working to improve efficiency and social, ethical, and environmental responsibility in the global supply chain.

EMS (Environmental Management System): a framework that assists companies in establishing control over operations in order to lessen their environmental impacts and increase overall efficiency.

ESG (Environmental, Social, and Governance): a general term used to describe the three primary areas of import for companies focused on making their operations sustainable. These three performance dimensions are often highlighted and evaluated by companies in their sustainability reports.

EVP (Employee Volunteer Program): a type of program that aims to engage employees while helping the local community.

FASB (Financial Accounting Standards Board): a private, not-for-profit organization that develops the financial accounting standards for the private sector in the United States.

FSC (Forest Stewardship Council): an independent, nonprofit membership organization that protects forests by setting standards for responsible forest management under which forests and companies are certified.

GAAP (Generally Accepted Accounting Principles): a set of concepts developed by the Financial Accounting Standards Board that determine how organizations in the United States prepare, present, and report their financial statements.

GASB (Governmental Accounting Standards Board): an independent organization that establishes and improves standards of accounting and financial reporting for U.S. state and local governments.

GHGs (Greenhouse Gases): gases that trap heat in the atmosphere causing the greenhouse effect that supports life on earth, but that can have dangerous effects if their concentrations increase too much.

GHG Protocol (Greenhouse Gas Protocol): an international accounting tool for businesses and governmental organizations to track, calculate, and manage their greenhouse gas emissions. The protocol almost always serves as the benchmark for other greenhouse gas standards developed throughout the world.

GIIN (Global Impact Investing Network): a nonprofit organization that works to increase the scale and effectiveness of impact investments, which are investments made in companies, organizations, and funds with the purpose of creating positive social and environmental impact in addition to financial return.

GIIRS (Global Impact Investing Ratings System): a ratings system that measures the social and environmental impact of companies and funds. GIIRS likens its assessment system to that of Morningstar investment rankings and Capital IQ financial analytics.

GISR (Global Initiative for Sustainability Ratings): an initiative whose mission is to design a generally accepted ratings framework for assessing the sustainability performance of companies.

GRI (Global Reporting Initiative): a nonprofit organization that works toward a sustainable global economy by providing sustainability reporting assistance, specifically their widely known Sustainability Reporting Framework.

GSA (General Services Administration): a federal agency that provides and maintains buildings, acquires goods and services, and promotes administrative best practices and efficient operations for the U.S. government.

HIP (Human Impact and Profit): a measurement and management tool that quantifies the products, services, operations and management practices of sustainability and citizenship, and is used both by corporations and investors.

IIRC (International Integrated Reporting Council): an international coalition of regulators, investors, companies, standard setters, accounting professionals, and NGOs that seeks to create the most commonly used framework for corporate reporting. Their "integrated report" method encourages companies to consider all aspects of an organization in reporting (strategy, governance, performance, and prospects), to increase their value creation over the short, medium, and long term.

ISO (International Organization for Standardization): a Swiss based organization that brings together representatives from around the world to agree on voluntary international standards for products, services, and good practice, seeking to make businesses more effective and efficient.

IRIS (Impact Reporting and Investment Standards): established by the Global Impact Investing Network (see GIIN), these performance standards are used by impact investors to determine and evaluate the social, environmental, and financial success of impact investments and the impact investment industry at large.

IVA (Intangible Value Assessment): a tool that assesses companies' financially material risks and opportunities arising from environmental, social, and governance factors.

KPI (Key Performance Indicator): areas of measurement by which companies can track their performance in relation to their business objectives, often utilizing target goals or ranges as benchmarks for future evaluation.

L3C (Low-profit Limited Liability Company): a company focusing principally on charitable or educational goals that may make a small profit, as long as making a profit is not the primary purpose of the organization. L3Cs are often considered hybrid organizations between nonprofit and for profit entities.

LCA (Life Cycle Assessment): a measurement of the potential environmental aspects and impacts of any organization, product, or service. This assessment evaluates every stage of development, allowing for a "cradle to grave" estimation of environmental effects.

MDGs (Millennium Development Goals): eight objectives officially established by the United Nations in 2000, from the eradication of extreme poverty, to the advancement of environmental sustainability, to halting the spread of HIV/AIDs; all to be met by a target date of 2015.

NCA (Natural Capital Accounting): a type of accounting that measures the indispensable resources and benefits essential for human survival and economic activity provided by the ecosystem. Natural capital is commonly divided into renewable resources (agricultural crops, vegetation, and wildlife) and nonrenewable resources (fossil fuels and mineral deposits).

NGO (Nongovernmental Organization): a not-for-profit group, principally independent from government, which is organized on a local, national, or international level to address issues in support of the public good.

OECD (Organization for Economic Cooperation and Development): a global organization of representatives from 34 member countries that meets to advance ideas and review progress in specific policy areas, such as economics, trade, science, employment, education, and financial markets.

PRI (Principles for Responsible Investment): the six principles of responsible investing supported by institutional investors who believe that environmental, social, and corporate governance issues can affect the performance of investment portfolios.

SASB (Sustainability Accounting Standards Board): a nonprofit organization engaged in the development and dissemination of industry-specific sustainability accounting standards in the United States.

SDGs (Sustainable Development Goals): The SDGs are the central UN platform for the follow-up and review of the 2030 Agenda for Sustainable Development adopted at the United Nations Sustainable Development Summit on 25 September 2015.

SRI (Socially Responsible Investing): values-based asset portfolio management.

SROI (Social Return on Investment): a method to quantify and monetize the social value created by an organization's programs, especially those in the nonprofit sector. This process was created by an American company, REDF, in the 1990s and is widely used today.

SSRN (Social Science Research Network): an organization devoted to the worldwide distribution of social science research, comprised of a number of specialized networks in each of the social sciences.

TBL (Triple Bottom Line): a term, created by SustainAbility founder John Elkington in the 1990s, encapsulating three particular assessment areas by which businesses and investors should measure value: economic, social, and environmental.

UNGC (United Nations Global Compact): a global initiative established in 2000 that provides a principle-based framework for businesses to adopt more sustainable and socially responsible policies in the areas of human rights, labor standards, anti-corruption, and the environment.

UNPRI (United Nations Principles of Responsible Investing): a United Nations supported initiative convening investors to put the six principles of responsible investing into practice through investment decision-making and ownership practices.

REFERENCES

Becker-Olsen, K. L., Cudmore, B. A., & Hill, R. P. (2006). The impact of perceived corporate social responsibility on consumer behavior. *Journal of Business Research*, *59*(1), 46–53.

Bennett, G., & Williams, F. (2011). *Mainstream green: Moving sustainability from niche to normal (4)*. Ogilvy & Mather.

Boone, J. B., McKechnie, S., & Swanberg, J. (2011). Predicting employee engagement in an age-diverse retail workforce. *Journal of Organizational Behavior*, *32*, 173–196.

Boston College Center for Corporate Citizenship. (2015). *Community involvement study 2015*. Boston, MA: Trustees of Boston College.

Boston College Center for Corporate Citizenship. (2017). *The state of corporate citizenship 2014*. Boston, MA: Trustees of Boston College.

Delmas, M. A., Etzion, D., & Nairn-Birch, N. (2013). Triangulating environmental performance: What do corporate social responsibility ratings really capture? *The Academy of Management Perspectives*, *27*(3), 255–267.

Department of the Treasury. United States Internal Revenue Service Publication 526 Cat. No. 15050A.

Department of the Treasury. United States Internal Revenue Service Publication 4221-PF (Rev. 8-2014) Cat. No. 49830S.

Dimson, E., Karakaş, O., & Li, X. (2015). Active ownership. *Review of Financial Studies, 28*(12), 3225–3268.

Edelman. (2013). *2013 Edelman Trust Barometer*. Chicago, IL: Edelman.

EU Directive 2014/95, Retrieved from: http://eur-lex.europa.eu/legal-content/EN/TXT/?uri=CELEX%3A32014L0095

Galbraith, J., Downey, D., & Kates, A. (2001). *Designing dynamic organizations: A hands-on guide for leaders at all levels*. AMACOM Division of the American Management Association.

Gallup. (2013). *State of the global workplace: Employee engagement insights for business leaders worldwide*. Washington, DC: Gallup.

Gardberg, N. A., & Fombrun, C. J. (2006). Corporate citizenship: Creating intangible assets across institutional environments. *Academy of Management Review, 31*(2), 329–346.

Grant, A. M., Dutton, J. E., & Rosso, B. D. (2008).Giving commitment: Employee support programs and the prosocial sensemaking process. *Academy of Management Journal, 51*(5), 898–918.

Green House Gasses Protocol, http://www.ghgprotocol.org/standards/corporate-standard

Intel Corporation. (2004). *Everything matters: Global citizenship report 2003*. Intel, Santa Clara.

Jones, D. A. (2010). Does serving the community also serve the company? Using organizational identification and social exchange theories to understand employee responses to a volunteerism programme. *Journal of Occupational and Organizational Psychology, 83*(4), 857–878.

Jones, D., Willness, C., & Madey S. (2014). Why are job seekers attracted by corporate social performance? Experimental and field tests of three signal–based mechanisms. *Academy of Management Journal*, 57(2), 383–404.

KPMG, (2010). Intangible Assets and Goodwill in the Context of Business Combinations: An Industry Study, Advisory, KPMG AG Wirtschaftsprüfungsgesellschaft, a subsidiary of KPMG Europe LLP and a member firm of the KPMG network.

Lawrence, R. G. (2004). Framing obesity the evolution of news discourse on a public health issue. *The Harvard International Journal of Press/Politics*, 9(3), 56–75.

Margolis, J. D., Elfenbein, H. A., & Walsh, J. P. (2007). Does it pay to be good? A meta-analysis and redirection of research on the relationship between corporate social and financial performance. Ann Arbor, 1001, 48109-1234.

Marquis, C., & Villa, L. V. (2012). *Managing stakeholders with corporate social responsibility*. Oxford: Harvard Business School Publishings.

New York Times, (2005). Retrieved from: http://www.nytimes.com/2005/02/20/business/yourmoney/you-want-any-fruit-with-that-big-mac.html?_r=0

New York Times. (2016). Laurence D. Fink's 2016 Corporate Governance Letter. *New York Times*, February 2. Retrieved from http://www.nytimes.com/interactive/2016/02/02/business/dealbook/document-larry-finks-2016-corporate-governance-letter.html?_r=0

Orlitzky, M., Schmidt, F. L., Rynes, S. L., (2003). Corporate social and financial performance: A meta-analysis. *Organization Studies*, 24(3), 403.

Raffaelli, R., & Glynn, M. A. (2014).Turnkey or tailored? Relational pluralism, institutional complexity, and the organizational adoption of more or less customized practices. *Academy of Management Journal*, 57(2), 541–562.

Raithel, S., Wilczynski, P., Schloderer, M. P., & Schwaiger, M. (2010).The value-relevance of corporate reputation during the financial crisis. *Journal of Product & Brand Management*, *19*(6), 389–400.

Research Magazine (2003). Most Widely Held Stock throughout the Socially Responsible Fund Industry. Retrieved from http://csrreportbuilder.intel.com/PDFfiles/archived_reports/Intel%202003%20CSR%20Report.pdf 2003 Report, page 38.

Simmons, C. J., & Becker-Olsen, K. L. (2006). Achieving marketing objectives through social sponsorships. *Journal of Marketing*, *70*(4), 154–169.

The Consumer Goods Forum, For a full list visit http://www.theconsumergoodsforum.com/about-the-forum/our-members

Lawrence, R. G. (2004). Framing obesity: the evolution of news discourse on a public health issue. *The Harvard International Journal of Press/Politics*, *9*, 56.

The Hindu, (2015). *The Hindu*, September 13, Retrieved from: http://www.thehindu.com/business/mcdonalds-india-to-double-outlets-by-2020/article7648207.ece

Thomas, M. L., Fraedrich, J. P., & Mullen, L. G. (2011). Successful cause-related marketing partnering as a means to aligning corporate and philanthropic goals: an empirical study. *Academy of Marketing Studies Journal*, *15*(2), 113.

U.S. Department of Energy *U.S. HEV sales by Model (1999-2013)*. Alternative Fuels and Advanced Vehicle Data Center (U.S. DoE). Retrieved from http://www.afdc.energy.gov/data/10301

U.S. Environmental Protection Agency (2012). Sustainability Concepts in Decision-Making: Tools and Approaches for the US Environmental Protection Agency 2012, 26.

U.S. Environmental Protection Agency, Retrieved from: https://www.epa.gov/research/methods-models-tools-and-databases

Vitaliano, D. F. (2010).Corporate social responsibility and labor turnover. Corporate Governance. *The International Journal of Business in Society, 10*(5), 563–573.

Winterich, K. P., Mittal, V., & Aquino, K. (2013). When Does Recognition Increase Charitable Behavior? Toward a Moral Identity-Based Model. *Journal of Marketing, 77,* 121–134.

World Business Council for Sustainable Development, Retrieved from http://www.wbcsd.org/publications-and-tools.aspx

Zakaria, F. (2007). Cathedral thinking, concept first introduced by former Duke Energy Chairman and CEO James E. Rogers in: 'Cathedral Thinking:' Energy's Future. *Newsweek*, August 20/27.

INDEX